The Inside Game

William B. Mead

A
BOOK

The Inside Game

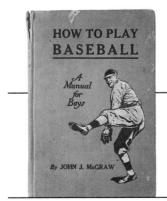

When the dugout empties, a manager's game plan goes into
action. A manager's job is to give his players an edge wherever
possible, and if the players were Baltimore Orioles under Earl
Weaver, they were already one step ahead of the opposition by
the time they took the field. Stressing pitching, defense and
power, Weaver led the Orioles to 16 winning seasons in 17
years. His only sub-.500 season—1986—was his last.

Weaver's Way

Earl Weaver was a miser. As manager of the Baltimore Orioles, he hoarded his pinch hitters, waiting to send them in at just the right moment. In the 1979 World Series against Pittsburgh, Weaver tried to save his left-handed pinch hitters to use against Kent Tekulve, the Pirates' right-handed sidearming bullpen ace. In the eighth inning of Game 4, he got his chance. The Pirates were ahead, 6–3, but Kiko Garcia singled to lead off the Baltimore eighth. Ken Singleton followed with another single and was forced at second on a fielder's choice that put Eddie Murray on first. Doug DeCinces walked, loading the bases, and the Pittsburgh manager, Chuck Tanner, brought in Tekulve.

Whereupon Weaver sent in three straight left-handed pinch hitters. John Lowenstein doubled into the right field corner, scoring two runs and leaving runners at second and third. Billy Smith was walked intentionally. Terry Crowley doubled into the right field corner, scoring two more runs. Weaver let pitcher Tim Stoddard bat—he wanted Stoddard to pitch—and he singled through a drawn-in infield, bringing home the inning's fifth run. The sixth scored on a force play, and the Orioles won, 9–6.

The Pirates came back to win that World Series, Tekulve saving Game 7. But Weaver was still on top, still considered baseball's best manager. As a strategist, he is widely regarded as one of history's best. His record reflects his skills. Over 17 seasons, Weaver managed Baltimore to six American League East championships, four pennants and one world championship.

When Baltimore manager Earl Weaver wasn't figuring out a new way to win games, he was usually screaming at umpires. One of his favorites was Ron Luciano (opposite, right). Once, Luciano ejected Weaver from four straight games.

For 17 years, Weaver called all the shots for the Orioles, and they were invariably in focus. He led his team to five 100-win seasons, one more than the legendary John McGraw did with the New York Giants. Only the Yankees' Joe McCarthy has more with six.

Weaver's basic strategy was simple, or at least he would have you believe it was. Send out a good pitcher, put some guys in the lineup who can hit the ball over the fence, sit back and wait for home runs to score runs in clusters. Yet Weaver knew that a winning team had to take every advantage it could. So he made sure his team gave away very few runs—none, if Weaver had his way—while stealing as many runs as possible from opponents. Earl Weaver didn't think much of stealing bases, but if a trick double-steal play might win one game a season, it was worth learning, and learning well.

Under Weaver, the Orioles learned everything well. Jim Palmer, the regal Hall of Fame pitcher who had eight 20-win seasons under Weaver, used to curse the spring training drills that he and the rest of the team had to go through. Over and over, the batter hit to the right side, the pitcher covered first, and the first baseman fielded the ball and tossed it to the pitcher for the out. Whether the pitcher was Jim Palmer, the Cy Young celebrity, or some aspiring youngster, the drill was the same, and it was rigorously repeated. Next might come hits to left field with runners on, say, first and third. Who takes the cutoff? Does the pitcher back up third or back up home?

Weaver made sure the Orioles *knew,* and he made sure his stars worked as hard on these mundane drills as did the rookies. With stars like Palmer, Frank and Brooks Robinson, and Eddie Murray drilling hard and dripping sweat in the hot Florida sunshine, younger players were rarely tempted to slack off. When they did, they heard from the abrasive Weaver or one of his coaches, and they usually found themselves on the bench or back in the Orioles' minor league camp.

Weaver knew the book, but he also used his common sense, adapting the old strategic verities to modern playing conditions. Perhaps more

The Orioles made a mockery of the first three AL Championship Series, outscoring their opponents 58–22 in three consecutive sweeps—two over Minnesota and one over Oakland. In 1970 right fielder Frank Robinson (20) and pitcher Pete Richert gave Weaver his second ALCS victory bath.

Hall of Famer Jim Palmer had a stormy relationship with Weaver. "Jimmy likes to help me manage," Weaver said, but the Orioles' skipper did allow Palmer to position his fielders (above) based on what he was going to throw.

than any other manager, Earl Weaver bridged baseball's generation gap of field leadership. Weaver was trained in the old school. In 1948, at the age of 17, he signed a minor league contract with the St. Louis Cardinals. It was a dream come true for young Weaver, whose father ran a dry cleaning business in St. Louis and often sent his son into the clubhouse with fresh uniforms for the Cardinal players. But Weaver never made it to the Cardinal clubhouse as a player; though his playing career lasted ten years, he played all of them in the minors.

In 1956 Weaver was playing second base for a lousy, last-place team in Knoxville, Tennessee. He was asked to manage the team for the season's last few weeks. He did it, assuming it would be his last fling in baseball. The Orioles rescued him with a $3,500 offer to manage a Class D farm team the next season.

Weaver managed in the minors for another ten years. His teams won three pennants and never finished lower than fourth. But no one gets famous in the minor leagues, and Weaver was virtually unknown when he finally made the majors in 1968 as an Oriole coach under manager Hank Bauer.

Bauer, a former Marine who had starred for the Yankees under Casey Stengel, barely spoke to Weaver. He suspected that the Orioles had put Weaver on the coaching staff as a manager in waiting, and he was right. At the 1968 All-Star break, the Orioles fired Bauer and replaced him with Weaver—a minor league nobody who, at 37, was the youngest manager in the AL.

But after 20 seasons in the minors, Weaver was hardly green. As a marginal player, he had absorbed the game, learning every angle in the hope that his savvy could get him to the majors. As a player, it didn't; as a manager, it

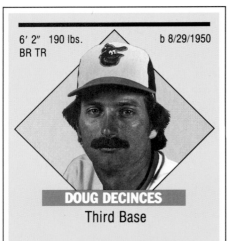

6' 2" 190 lbs. b 8/29/1950
BR TR

DOUG DECINCES

Third Base

It's hard to imagine the kind of pressure Doug DeCinces was under when he stepped into retiring Oriole Brooks Robinson's impossibly large cleats at third base. Unfavorable comparisons were made, and not just at the ballpark. When DeCinces dropped peas from his fork, dinner guests said, "Brooksy would have had it."

Beginning in 1976, his first year as Baltimore's full-time third baseman, DeCinces had a roller coaster career in Baltimore. He hit .286 with 28 homers in 1978 but followed that with a .230 average in 1979. To complicate matters, he had chronic back problems and a habit of catching ground balls with his face. His oft-restructured nose, broken for the fifth time in 1979, earned him the nickname "the Horn."

It was not until DeCinces was traded to the California Angels in 1982 that he had his best year, hitting .301 with 30 home runs and 97 RBI. Twice that season he slugged three home runs in a single game.

Even with his injuries, DeCinces averaged 80 RBI and 22 home runs in six seasons with the Angels. His fielding also improved at Anaheim, and occasionally, he found himself compared favorably with Brooks Robinson. "DeCinces does all the routine stuff," said teammate Brian Downing, "and every once in a while throws a guy out from the hole while horizontal."

Second baseman Davey Johnson played on three of Weaver's AL champions, then—with a strong nod to Weaver's methods—won two NL East titles as manager of the New York Mets. Johnson's Mets won at least 90 games a season from 1985 to 1989.

did. He knew he could evaluate talent, call plays and use his bench. He had no doubt that he could manage in the major leagues. "Many of the most successful managers had been mediocre ballplayers like myself because those of us with limited abilities had to think more and play smart baseball to sustain a professional playing career on any level," Weaver said.

The Orioles were far behind the Tigers when Weaver took over in 1968, and they failed to catch Detroit, finishing second. But in 1969 Baltimore took first place on April 16 and never slipped to second, winning the AL East by 19 games and finishing with 109 wins, third in league history. The 1954 Indians won 111, the 1927 Yankees, 110. In 1970 the Orioles won 108 games, leaving second-place New York 15 games back, and in 1971 they won 101 and finished 12 games ahead of the Tigers. League championship series were then three-out-of-five affairs, and Baltimore swept all three series, winning nine straight games to dispatch the Minnesota Twins in 1969 and 1970 and the Oakland Athletics in 1971.

The Orioles won just one of those three World Series. Still, it was quite a start for young Weaver. Fans weren't sure how much credit he deserved, because the Orioles had a great team. In 1969 Boog Powell, the Baltimore first baseman, hit 37 homers, while Frank Robinson hit 32, Paul Blair 26 and Brooks Robinson 23. The Oriole lineup was powerful, and the pitching and defense were beyond belief. Brooks Robinson is usually rated as the best defensive third baseman in history. Mark Belanger was a superb shortstop, Davey Johnson—more recently manager of the New York Mets—was a fine second baseman, and Paul Blair was an outstanding center fielder. Pitchers Mike Cuellar and Dave McNally both won 20 or more games all three sea-

sons. Jim Palmer won 16, 20 and 20. In 1971 the Orioles had four 20-game winners, as Pat Dobson joined Cuellar, McNally and Palmer.

Still, it was Weaver who stitched the pieces together, and he started by working out a meticulous training schedule for his first spring training in 1969—one that kept every player busy. Weaver and his coaches also laid down a detailed manual of fundamentals, to be used throughout the Oriole system. If the right cutoff man is always at the right spot, and the right player is always backing up third or home, runs are saved—and games are won. "If you can devise five plays in which you can get, say, three game-winning outs on each over a season, that gives you fifteen ball games that you wouldn't otherwise have won," Weaver wrote in his autobiography. "Fifteen extra victories in a season can certainly mean the difference in a pennant race." Weaver's theories worked. In 1970, for example, the Orioles won 40 and lost only 15 of those games decided by a single run.

Weaver was cold-blooded in his evaluation of talent, and he got the most from every player. Mike Torrez, a good pitcher who happened to get traded frequently, pitched for 18 seasons and won 20 games just once: for Weaver's Orioles, in 1975. Weaver studied Torrez, saw that he needed a slow curve to round out his repertoire and had Baltimore's excellent pitching coach, George Bamberger, teach Torrez the pitch. Similarly, Pat Dobson pitched in the majors for 11 years, yet won 20 games only under Weaver. Ditto Steve Stone: 11 seasons, four clubs, one 20-game season. In fact, Stone won 25 and the Cy Young Award for Baltimore in 1980. Dobson and Stone were curveball pitchers. Weaver taught them to rely on other pitches when their curves weren't working—to use the right pitch at the right time, often against the expectations of the batter.

When Weaver took over as the Orioles' manager in 1968, one of the job's benefits was having Frank Robinson in the lineup— and the dugout. Robinson was not only a great power hitter, but an outstanding competitor and team leader as well. In 1988 Robinson became manager of the Orioles.

Take Your Base

"Walks kill teams," said George Bamberger, Orioles pitching coach. In the battle for control over home plate, the Orioles inflicted most of the damage in each of Earl Weaver's 17 seasons as manager. The Orioles walked away from their opponents. Below is a comparison of walks allowed and received by the Orioles during the Weaver years from 1968 to 1982, and 1985 to 1986.

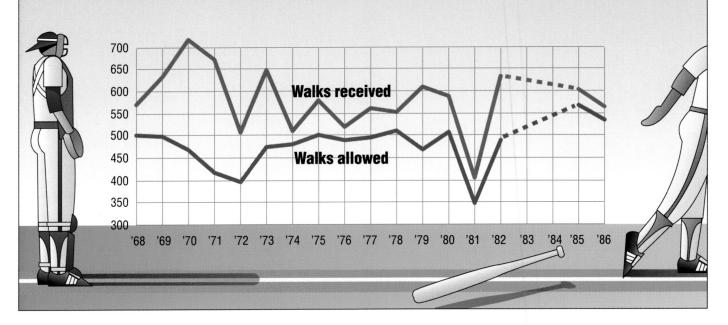

Weaver was a tough and temperamental boss who chewed out players for mistakes and ranted incessantly at umpires. Yet his managing was unemotional, logical and sophisticated. In Weaver's early years with the Orioles, it was still the custom to let starting pitchers go as long as they could. Sentiment was involved; it was considered cruel or unsportsmanlike to pull a pitcher who was working on a shutout, no matter how tired he might be. But Weaver had no truck with such traditions. If a reliever was more likely to protect a win, Weaver called him in. In a 1979 game he pulled Steve Stone, a right-hander, after 8⅔ innings of one-hit ball. The Orioles were one run ahead, Stone had just walked a batter and a strong left-handed hitter, Cecil Cooper, was due up for Milwaukee. Weaver brought in southpaw Tippy Martinez, who retired Cooper and saved Stone's victory.

Just as he angered Oriole fans by pulling pitchers, Weaver often angered opposing fans by pitching around their strong hitters. If a home run would beat the Orioles, he didn't mind walking power hitters. In 1969 Harmon Killebrew of Minnesota led the AL in homers with 49 and in RBI with 140. In the 1969 ALCS, the Orioles walked Killebrew every time he came up in a threatening situation. In the first two games, Killebrew drew five straight walks. He didn't hit a homer or drive in a run in the series, and the Twins didn't win a game.

Many players of limited ability languish on the bench. Weaver pinpointed their strengths and used them, while sheltering them from their own weaknesses by sitting them down against pitchers they couldn't handle. Pat Kelly, a journeyman outfielder whom the Orioles picked up before the 1977 season, was a hot spring hitter. Under Weaver,

Second baseman Rich Dauer (left, being upended by Boston's Jim Rice) was Weaver's kind of player—smart, tough and fundamentally sound. Dauer was no great threat at the plate, but his fielding was steady, and in 1978 he set major league records by playing 86 consecutive games and handling 425 consecutive chances without an error.

Catcher Elrod Hendricks did a lot for the Orioles under Weaver. He batted left-handed, was solid defensively, provided occasional power and helped translate for Spanish-speaking pitcher Mike Cuellar. In the late 1970s Hendricks became Weaver's bullpen coach.

Kelly was frequently in the lineup in April and May, before retiring to a part-time role. "Not everybody can be Mickey Mantle," Weaver told sportswriter Tom Boswell. "You have to be satisfied with players who have one or two tools and make the most of them." To play left field, Weaver made the most of John Lowenstein, a left-handed hitter acquired on waivers; Gary Roenicke, who batted right and was traded to the Orioles as a throw-in; and, occasionally, Benny Ayala, a right-handed hitter whom the Orioles picked up in a minor league trade. What a platoon! In 1979 the O's won the pennant as Roenicke and Lowenstein drove in 98 runs between them. By 1982 the Oriole trio led the league as Baltimore left fielders, put together, hit 41 homers and drove in 123 runs.

Weaver was one of the first managers to keep detailed statistics, and to use them in his managerial decisions. He knew how every player had performed against every pitcher, in every situation. He knew how many fastballs and how many curves Jim Palmer had thrown to Reggie Jackson, where they were in the strike zone, what Jackson had done with them, whether he had hit grounders, line drives or fly balls, and to what fields. Every now and then Weaver would make a confounding move. For example, he once sent up weak-hitting Mark Belanger to bat against Nolan Ryan. Belanger singled, and Weaver wasn't surprised. He had it on paper; Belanger, for whatever reason, owned Ryan.

Most managers are copycats, but Weaver was an innovator. In 1981 he forced a change in the rule book. At designated hitter he was platooning right-handed Benny Ayala with left-handed Terry Crowley. The Oriole DH usually batted sixth. This posed a problem. Let's say the Yankees started southpaw Tommy John. Ayala would be the Baltimore DH because he batted

Continued on page 16

Bobby Grich

I n a champagne-soaked locker room at Anaheim Stadium, California Angels second baseman Bobby Grich tried to express his emotions. It was September 1979, the Angels had just clinched the American League Western Division title and Grich had posted the best season of his career. "I've been an Angels fan since I was a kid," said Grich, who had grown up in southern California. "I'd sit in the stands and say, 'I'd like to be out there someday.' Now here I am. It's unbelievable."

Grich was first signed as a shortstop by the Baltimore Orioles in 1967, but breaking into their already talent-laden infield was no easy task. After a respectable but uninspired performance in 30 games in 1970, Grich was sent back to the Orioles AAA farm club with instructions to learn to hit with power. He got his lessons in the form of a book about Joe DiMaggio. "When I got to the part where the writer detailed, day by day, DiMaggio's 56-game hitting streak," Grich recalled, "it knocked me out, how this guy hit doubles, home runs, triples—almost nothing but long shots." Using photos and films of DiMaggio as a guide, Grich began imitating DiMaggio's wide stance. The payoff was immediate. In 1971 Grich led the International League with a .336 average, 32 homers and 124 runs. He was named league MVP. The Orioles had no choice but to make room for him full-time in 1972.

A rookie at last, Grich became the ultimate utility infielder. He played 81 games at shortstop, 45 at second base, 16 at first and 8 at third. Seemingly unfazed by the constant shifting, he hit .278 with 12 homers and made his first of six trips to the All-Star game. The following season, 1973, the Orioles gave

Grich a permanent home at second base, and he thanked them by setting the major league record for highest fielding average by a second baseman—.995—making only five errors in 162 games. That year also marked the first of four straight seasons in which he led the AL in putouts and three in which he led in assists.

But Grich's hitting seemed to stagnate. Ten to 20 homers a year and averages in the .260s aren't bad numbers, but manager Earl Weaver had said that he would be "really disappointed" if Grich never hit .300 with 25 home runs. Grich never posted those numbers for Weaver, and when he was granted free agency after the 1976 season, he signed with his hometown favorite, the Angels.

Just when everything seemed to be going Grich's way—he got a five-year, $1.5 million contract from baseball's Santa Claus, Angels owner Gene Autry—he injured his back. He missed almost all of the 1977 season and was barely effective in 1978, but Grich was determined to make amends. He began an ambitious weight-lifting program and studied teammate Rod Carew's batting stroke, emulating his light grip on the bat and relaxed style at the plate. By midseason the white elephant the Angels had purchased turned into a gold mine. In 1979 Grich batted .294 with 30 home runs and 101 RBI.

His final outstanding performance came in the strike-tainted 1981 split season, when Grich tied for the AL home run title with 22 and led the league in slugging average with .543. Grich played with the Angels until he retired after the 1986 season, and he is still the all-time single-season record-holder for fielding percentage among second basemen.

BOBBY GRICH

Second Base
Baltimore Orioles 1970-1976
California Angels 1977-1986

GAMES	2,008
AT-BATS	6,890
BATTING AVERAGE	
Career	.266
Season High	.304
SLUGGING AVERAGE	
Career	.424
Season High	.543
HITS	
Career	1,833
Season High	157
DOUBLES	
Career	320
Season High	31
TRIPLES	
Career	47
Season High	7
HOME RUNS	
Career	224
Season High	30
TOTAL BASES	2,919
EXTRA-BASE HITS	591
RUNS BATTED IN	
Career	864
Season High	101
RUNS	
Career	1,033
Season High	93

Bobby Grich had his most potent seasons at the plate on the West Coast with the Angels, but he won all four of his Gold Gloves on the East Coast with the Orioles.

Oriole shortstop Mark Belanger may have been the most valuable .228 hitter in baseball history. The 18-year veteran won eight Gold Gloves, and his work ethic never faltered—he took 60 to 100 ground balls every day in practice.

right-handed. But if the Orioles knocked out John in the first inning, the Yanks might bring in righty Ron Davis in relief, forcing Weaver to pinch-hit Crowley for Ayala, who would be lost for the game. So Weaver started writing in pitcher Steve Stone as his DH. He never intended for Stone to bat—one night, in fact, Stone wasn't even on hand, having flown to the next stop so he would be rested to pitch. When Stone's turn to bat came up in the first or second inning, Weaver sent up either Ayala or Crowley to pinch-hit, depending on whether the opposing pitcher was right- or left-handed. Sacrilege! Almost immediately, Weaver's brainstorm was outlawed when the AL ruled that the DH must come to bat at least once.

Other Weaver innovations stuck. Belanger was a great shortstop but a weak hitter. In September, when rosters swell to 40 players, Weaver found a way to get one at-bat per game from a superior hitter, without losing Belanger's defensive skill. Weaver used the play only during away games when Baltimore was up first. He listed a better hitter in his starting lineup as leadoff man and shortstop. Royle Stillman filled that role in 1975 and went 4 for 9 as Belanger's stand-in. In the bottom of the first, Belanger took the field, and he batted in turn for the rest of the game.

In 1978 Weaver again shocked traditionalists. In Toronto one night, the Blue Jays cuffed Oriole pitching for 19 runs. The game was lost, but Weaver's exhausted pitchers still had to work the final couple of innings, which would stretch the staff thin for the next few days. Weaver saw a way out. He sent in outfielder Larry Harlow to pitch, followed by catcher Elrod Hendricks. The Jays scored four more runs, but so what? Weaver had saved at least one of his relief pitchers from a useless and tiring appearance. After the protests died down, other managers quietly copied the idea.

Weaver was one of the best at piecing together a good pitching staff, hiring excellent pitching coaches—first George Bamberger and then Ray Miller, both of whom became big-league managers —teaching his pitchers how to get the most from their ability and pacing his staff so his starters did not wear out late in the season. Today, most teams use a five-man pitching rotation. Weaver preferred to use four starters, with a fifth for doubleheaders and other spot starts. You would think Oriole starters would have worn down, but they didn't. Year after year, Baltimore played its best baseball late in the season. In 1970 McNally, Cuellar and Palmer started 23 games in August, pitched 15 complete games and went 18–2. In 1974 the Orioles, trailing Boston by eight games on August 29, won 28 of their last 34 games. They ran off ten straight wins, including five straight shutouts and 54 straight scoreless innings—AL records. They clinched the pennant on the second-to-last day of the season. In 1982 they won 27 of 32 games from August 19 to September 20, making up 7½ games to tie Milwaukee with one game to go. The Brewers won it, beating Palmer in the final game of his last great season.

In Weaver's first 13 years as Baltimore manager, the O's had at least one 20-game winner every season, 22 in all. To be sure, the pitchers were talented, the Oriole defense was superb and the team scored runs. Still, no other team in this century has boasted a 20-game winner that many seasons in a row. Weaver, with the active help of his coaches, never hesitated to tell a pitcher what he had to do to improve. Some pitchers rebelled. "When a pitcher won't listen, you let him get beat," Weaver said. "After it happens, you sit a pitcher down and ask if he wants to be a loser all his life."

Pitcher Dave McNally added an extra run to Weaver's favorite play—the three-run homer—with a grand slam (above) off Cincinnati's Wayne Granger in Game 3 of the 1970 World Series. It was McNally's second career Series homer and vaulted the O's to a 9–3 win.

Doing the little things right was a hallmark of Weaver's Orioles, and one of the best at it was Paul Blair. Blair was the best defensive center fielder of his era, had great speed and could turn in a mean hook slide (above, avoiding the tag of Boston's Elston Howard).

Weaver is famous—or notorious—for his angry arguments with Jim Palmer, but in fact Weaver put his pitchers in charge of the game. He taught them to pitch their best, instructed them thoroughly on how best to pitch to that day's opposing team and then let them call their own game. Of course, the catcher gave signals. But Weaver encouraged his pitchers to use their own judgment, to shake off the catcher when they wanted to. He even encouraged them to move defensive players around, a practice Palmer perfected. After all, Weaver reasoned, the pitcher knew what pitches he was going to throw and where, so he should know where batters were likely to hit the ball and where infielders and outfielders should station themselves to catch it.

And the Orioles were darned good at catching it. Fans recall spectacular plays by Brooks Robinson, particularly in the 1970 World Series against Cincinnati. Belanger was almost as good at shortstop, and the Orioles boasted other fine defensive players: Davey Johnson and Bobby Grich at second base, Eddie Murray at first, Paul Blair and Frank Robinson in the outfield, Rick Dempsey behind the plate, Palmer on the mound. Oriole players won 35 Gold Gloves under Weaver, and Oriole teams finished first or second in fielding percentage 13 of Weaver's 17 seasons. "To me a great fielder is one who makes all the plays look simple," Weaver said. Weaver's meticulous records helped Baltimore fielders play in the right spot and anticipate likely events. His infielders took hundreds of practice grounders; at least 50 a night during the season.

Weaver was always looking for an edge. In 1969, his first full season as Baltimore's manager, he was puzzled by the outstanding infield play of opposing teams and surprised that his own infielders, who had the reputation

Baltimore's Doug DeCinces had to be tough to succeed the legendary Brooks Robinson at third base. In the 1979 World Series he took out Pirate second baseman Phil "Scrap Iron" Garner.

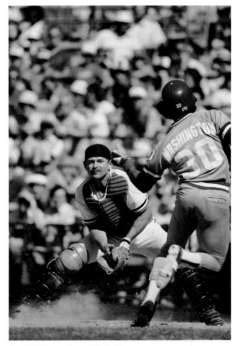

In 1976 catcher Rick Dempsey came to Baltimore as a throw-in in a ten-player trade and went on to catch more games than anyone else in Oriole history. His steadiness behind the plate helped Weaver harvest another fine crop of starting pitchers, including Mike Flanagan, Scott McGregor and Dennis Martinez.

of being tops in the league on defense, appeared to have no home field advantage. "For weeks I'd watch our infield of Brooks Robinson, Mark Belanger and Davey Johnson make nothing but routine stops while the other teams were robbing us blind," he told writer Tom Boswell. "Finally I realized that our great infielders didn't need the help. Only the other teams were benefiting from the high grass. So we mowed it low. All of a sudden our guys were making the great plays and other teams couldn't quite get to the ground balls. My first three years, we won over 100 games every year, and cutting the grass might have been the only smart thing I did."

Weaver's managerial logic came through most clearly in his offensive strategy. In his book *Weaver on Strategy* he wrote: "The power of the home run is so elementary that I fail to comprehend why people try to outsmart this game in other ways. If I were to play a singles hitter in right field or left field or at third base, he'd have to hit well over .300 and get on base often to be as valuable as a 25-homer man."

Baltimore's Memorial Stadium is a good home run ballpark. In the AL East, so are Yankee Stadium, Tiger Stadium and Boston's Fenway Park. On the whole, the AL has more ballparks with short fences than does the NL. So the home run offense is more prevalent in the AL—partly, perhaps, because Weaver preached its virtues so loudly and won so many championships. A slap hitter during his own playing days, Weaver liked the power offense and had the players and the ballparks to make it work.

In general, Weaver spurned the tactics of "scientific baseball." As he put it, "My outlook on the bunt has never changed. It's an out you're giving to the opposition, and no one is even certain that the bunt will be successful. If

6' 4" 210 lbs.   b 6/10/1947
BB TR

KEN SINGLETON
Outfield

As Ken Singleton came to bat during a spring training matchup, Baltimore pitching coach Ray Miller recalled that Singleton had predicted the pitcher "will throw a fastball away on the first pitch and if it's not a strike, he'll go high 2–0 and then throw the change-up." Singleton was right, said Miller, and "Kenny hit the change-up off the wall for a double."

With the Orioles from 1975 to 1984, the switch-hitting Singleton did more than out-think opposing pitchers. His quick bat turned pitches that were practically in the catcher's mitt into line drives. From 1977 to 1980 he hit 103 homers and was one of the best judges of balls and strikes in the league. His good eye, combined with consistent .300 hitting, helped him set several all-time Oriole records: 118 walks in 1975, a .328 batting average in 1977, and a .442 on-base percentage in 1977.

But Singleton ran as if the basepaths were covered in deep sand, and fans put their hands over their eyes when he went for extra bases. He had a solid glove in right field, but arm trouble and lack of speed landed him a permanent role as a designated hitter in the last years of his career. He did bunt for hits just twice in his 15-year career; he said, "The other team was 1,000 percent surprised."

Singleton called it quits in 1984. In 15 major-league seasons, the man Earl Weaver called "the most intelligent hitter I've ever seen" posted 2,029 hits, 1,065 RBI, 246 home runs and a .282 lifetime average.

Boog Powell swung a big bat—339 homers—but not as big as his appetite. "Sometimes when you're driving, the car just seems to turn by itself into a McDonald's," he said.

you play for one run, that's all you'll get." Weaver thought ahead, and he knew that a bunt might take the bat away from his best hitter. Say the score is tied and your leadoff man walks to open the ninth. You bunt him to second —whereupon the opposing pitcher walks your best hitter to set up a double play. Better, Weaver reasoned, to let the second hitter swing away.

As for the hit-and-run, Weaver called it "the worst play in baseball." He didn't even have a sign for it. The play is a waste, Weaver argued, because the batter is obliged to swing at the pitch, no matter how bad it is. So the batter is likely to be out. If he misses, the runner is usually thrown out at second. "You often give the opposition an out on the hit-and-run play," said Weaver, who hated to donate outs to the opposition. Weaver used a variation called the run-and-hit, in which the runner goes hell-for-leather attempting to steal second base, and the batter swings if he likes the pitch. The play is less risky.

Most years, the Orioles didn't steal many bases, and you can guess why. "The failed stolen base can be destructive, particularly at the top of the order, because it takes a runner off the basepaths ahead of your home-run hitters," Weaver said. But his devotion to power baseball did not overcome his sense of reality. In 1973 the Orioles lacked power, so Weaver went to the running game. The Orioles got 53 bunt hits and actually led the league in stolen bases with 146; they had some speedsters in Paul Blair, Rich Coggins and Al Bumbry. In 1974 Weaver was again forced to run, and the Orioles led their division in stolen bases. They won division championships both seasons. Yet Weaver still considered a running offense nothing more than a desperation strategy: "I've managed and won with guys who hit singles and stole bases, but I'd much rather have a power club. Those home runs make life a lot easier," he said.

Weaver liked to get men on base, hoping they would trot home as someone homered. So he treasured the base on balls: ranting against it to his pitchers, teaching its virtues to his batters. In the 1982 pennant race the Orioles lacked a good third baseman, and Weaver surprised many observers by playing Glenn Gulliver, a marginal player who spent most of his career in the minors. Gulliver couldn't hit much; he batted just .200. But he had a good batting eye and walked so much that his on-base percentage was .363—29 hits and 37 walks in 50 games. Weaver batted him second in the lineup, ahead of RBI men Ken Singleton and Eddie Murray.

Davey Johnson recalled a time when he was due to bat late in a game with the score tied, the bases loaded and two out. Weaver called Johnson back and sent up Tom Shopay to hit for him. Shopay was good at coaxing walks, and Weaver told him to get a walk. He did. Johnson didn't like being pulled, but the Orioles won.

"You can't worry about what is on the mind of the player who is being pinch-hit for," Weaver said. After all, he reasoned, if you fail to pinch-hit when the situation calls for it, your other players will be unhappy. Anyway, a manager's job is to win. In fact, Weaver was surprisingly old-school in his personal dealings with players. He rarely talked to them. If a player—even a star—got two "hellos" from Weaver in a month, he was lucky. When Belanger moved from the Orioles to the Dodgers in 1982, Tommy Lasorda confronted him during spring training and asked him why he never said "good morning" when he encountered his new manager. Belanger was pleasantly surprised. He had played 14 years under a manager who did not exchange greetings with his players. As the boss, Weaver liked to keep his distance. Besides, he reasoned, he could never promise a player anything. His way

In order for the Orioles to hit Weaver's beloved three-run homers, somebody had to get on base, and one of the greatest at it was Don Buford (above, sliding under the tag of Washington's Paul Casanova). Buford could play both the infield and the outfield, but his specialty was getting on base and scoring runs—he scored 99 runs each year from 1969 to 1971, all division-winning seasons for Baltimore.

For Earl Weaver (above, being tossed out by umpire Durwood Merrill, 33, while Oriole first baseman Eddie Murray, 33, looks on), his explosive behavior during games was part emotion, part calculation. "It actually took me a while to believe what a good game they'd give you the next night after a blowup," he said.

of patting a player on the back was to write his name on the lineup card. "A manager," he said, "must live by that hard-hearted cliché: what have you done for me today?"

Yet Weaver's players couldn't complain of rotting on the bench, because he had a role for everyone on the roster. He prided himself on "deep depth"—a bench better than good, with threatening left- and right-handed hitters ready to be sent up when the occasion arose. Bill Veeck, the colorful owner of the White Sox during Weaver's years with Baltimore, said this of Weaver: "When it comes to using his full 25-man squad, squeezing the most out of what each player can do and hiding their weaknesses, he's the best there is right now."

Weaver won his last pennant in 1979. After barely falling short of the division championship in 1980, 1981 and 1982, Weaver—an elder statesman at 52—retired to his favorite golf course in Florida. When the Orioles faltered in 1985, he was called out of retirement. But the team was weak and finished fourth in 1985 and seventh in 1986. That was enough for Weaver, who stepped down for good—until given a chance to manage in the Senior Professional League in 1989. The Orioles may have fallen short of the Weaver tradition in his final two seasons, but Earl was untarnished. As he used to say in the good years, "You're never as good as you look when you're winning and you're never as bad as you look when you're losing." The man was a philosopher. ◗◖

Mound Mentors

Traditionally, pitching coaches are known for three things: taking credit for good performances, denying responsibility for bad ones and telling the boys how much better pitchers were back when *they* were playing. But two Baltimore pitching coaches, George Bamberger and Ray Miller, tossed those traditions aside.

During their successive tenures as head pitching coach with the Orioles—Bamberger from 1968 to 1977 and Miller from 1978 to 1985—they helped ten pitchers win 20 games a season a total of 23 times. The pitching staff also collected six Cy Young Awards and produced at least one 20-game winner for 13 consecutive years.

The Oriole organization, dominated by Earl Weaver during those 18 years, practiced absolute uniformity of training methods from the big-league club down to the D-circuit minor league team. While Bamberger was guiding the big-league staff in the mid-1970s, Miller was using the same methods at Class AAA Rochester to coach future Oriole stars like Mike Flanagan and Scott McGregor. But it was Bamberger who built the peerless training system.

The cornerstone of Bamberger's method was physical conditioning. While many coaches prescribed complete rest for their pitchers between starts, Bamberger had his staff throw for a few minutes every day. He made them run until they weren't sure if they were in baseball or boot camp. The results: from 1968 to 1978 the Orioles led the American League in complete games six times, and their ace, Jim Palmer, led the league in innings pitched four times.

The Bamberger-Miller philosophy was simple. "There is nothing complicated about baseball," Bamberger said. "Throw strikes." Miller elaborated: "Work fast, throw strikes, and change speeds." The point was the same. Throw strikes to let the batter hit the ball, but change speeds so he can't hit it well. Then the superb Oriole fielders—who are on their toes because their pitcher is working fast—will snatch up everything that stays in the park. And even if the pitchers serve up a long ball or two, they'll probably be solo shots, because you don't give up walks when you're throwing strikes. The philosophy worked. The Orioles led the AL in ERA six times from 1969 to 1975, and were incredibly stingy with walks and hits. More important, from 1968 to 1985 they won seven division titles, five pennants and two world championships.

Bamberger and Miller were also experts at teaching maturity to players Miller described as "high-strung young thoroughbreds. They're young and we're trying to put an old head into a young body while not making it seem like brain surgery." The coaches didn't have to persuade stubborn young hurlers to follow their directions; the Orioles' bullpen products proved that they knew how to make a pitcher a star.

Pitcher Steve Stone was a prime example. Stone came to Baltimore in 1979 with a 67–72 record compiled over eight years with three different teams. In 1980 he went 25–7 and won the Cy Young Award. Stone doesn't need to be told the right pitching coach can make a difference. Let someone else tell stories about how much better pitchers were in the old days.

Oriole pitching coaches George Bamberger (above, top, with Earl Weaver) and Ray Miller (left, with Dennis Martinez) earned such outstanding reputations that each eventually became major league managers. Bamberger helped build the Milwaukee Brewers into contenders in the late 1970s, while Miller struggled in nearly two seasons with the Minnesota Twins in the mid-1980's.

Signals

Shaking the hand and slapping the butt of a player on the last leg of his home-run trot is a third-base coach's favorite job, and few brought more enthusiasm to the task than the Dodgers' Tommy Lasorda (above, with catcher Joe Ferguson).

Mixed signals are the worst signals, but that's apparently what a Red Sox runner got when Jim Rice (preceding page, right) gave the slide sign and Ed Jurak signalled him to come in standing up.

Baseball is not a mysterious game, but its system of signals mystifies most fans. Baseball signals, flashed in the open, are the diamond game's equivalent of the football huddle. They are the cement that binds individual players into coordinated team effort. "The game itself cannot begin without the catcher's first sign to the pitcher," says Jeff Torborg, manager of the Chicago White Sox. Without signals—without some means of communicating with players in the field—a manager's influence over game strategy would be sharply limited. Catchers would become receivers only. Pitchers, hitters and baserunners would be largely on their own, and mistakes would abound. Infield play would lose the smooth cohesion that has developed in recent years as strategies have improved to handle anticipated offensive plays—steal attempts, bunts and squeeze plays, the hit-and-run, the run-and-hit.

Like so much of baseball, signals go back more than a century. Probably the first manager to use them was Harry Wright, a cricketer who turned to baseball and became manager of the first openly professional team, the Cincinnati Red Stockings of 1869. Wright wanted his players to work together "like a nicely adjusted machine," and to achieve that kind of teamwork, he realized he had to communicate with his players—openly, but without the opposition catching on. So he invented hand signals. It was quite an innovation. Only 64 years before, the British Royal Navy had beaten Napoleon's French Navy in the Battle of Trafalgar with the use of a new weapon: coded signal flags that enabled Lord Nelson to coordinate the movements of his ships.

Managers, coaches and most players insist that baseball signals are simple. So is Spanish, to someone who has spoken it for years. To an

outsider—even a knowledgeable fan—signals are like a foreign language. Typically, a third-base coach has at least five signals he can give the batter: take the pitch, bunt, squeeze the runner home from third, hit-and-run, and steal. All but the "take" sign are signals to baserunners as well as to the hitter, and even the take sign gives the baserunner an edge he might use.

Five signals are not many; they're like a five-word vocabulary. Trouble is, each signal must be undecipherable to the other team, which employs coaches to figure out the opposition's signs. So third-base coaches go through a series of motions, disguising the real sign amid a flurry of bogus ones. Sometimes the whole presentation is a charade, a series of signs signifying nothing, designed only to confuse the opposition. The coach may have no message for the batter, or he might be pantomiming while the real signal comes from the dugout. If a coach really has a signal for the batter, he'll include in his motions a sign that is the "indicator" and another that is the "hot" signal. The indicator tells the batter that a subsequent sign is the one to act on—the hot signal.

The indicator might be a touch of the cap, a brush of the chin, a spoken word—almost anything. Typically, a coach might make five or six other motions before giving the indicator, and five or six more after giving the hot signal. If the bunt sign is, say, a raised thumb, the coach might raise his thumb twice *before* giving the indicator. In that case, the raised thumb means nothing; it is pure fakery. Only the sign *after* the indicator counts. The manager and coaches may set things up so the hot sign is the first sign after the indicator. The next day, or the next inning, it may be the third sign after the indicator. As long as players are kept posted—and everyone stays alert—small

Effective communication is never more essential than during a sacrifice bunt. Here, Padres second baseman Roberto Alomar indicates that there's no play at second base on Cubs catcher Rick Wrona (1), and for the player fielding the bunt to throw to first.

Milwaukee manager Tom Trebelhorn was never shy about going to his bullpen. When he wanted a lefty in the late 1980s, it was usually Dan Plesac, who averaged 29 saves a season from 1987 to 1989. But when he tapped his right arm it usually meant set-up man Chuck Crim, who led the AL in appearances in 1988 and 1989.

Correctly positioned outfielders can turn a double or triple into an easy out. If pitchers do their job, batters will likely hit the ball to where coaches like Oakland's Dave McKay have stationed the fielders.

changes in a team's signaling system can be made frequently enough to make sign stealing by the other team difficult, if not impossible.

Much the same system works between catcher and pitcher. The catcher flashes signs between his legs, and usually the signs are simple —such as one finger for a fastball, two for a curve, three for a change-up —because no one on the opposing team can see. A touch of the left thigh may call for a pitch on the left half of the plate, a touch of the right thigh for a pitch on the right half. With a runner on second, the catcher and pitcher usually go to a more sophisticated system, since the runner can see the catcher's signs. Many pitchers call their own games, or change the catcher's signs. For example, if the pitcher brushes his right leg with his glove, it might mean "move the number up one"—say, from one finger for a fastball to two fingers for a curve. When a pitcher shakes off his catcher, it may mean something and it may not. In baseball, several phony signals are given for every hot one. To further confuse the opposition, whoever is receiving the signal—the batter, a baserunner, the pitcher—has to give fake signals the same studious look he gives to hot signals, even continuing to look after getting the hot signal.

Managers and coaches try to keep their signaling systems as simple as they can. In All-Star games, they use very simple codes, since players have only one day to learn and the opposing team has only one day to break the code. For regular-season play, more deceptive systems are needed, because opposing teams can study the signals day after day. The simpler the code, the easier it is to break. The more complex the code, the easier it is for a player to miss a signal or to misinterpret one.

A runner on third base has an obstructed view of the home plate area, so if a pitch gets away from the catcher, the runner relies on the hitter for a sign as to whether or not to try to score. The Yankees' Willie Randolph (left) leaves no doubt as to his advice.

Sometimes a situation is so obvious that players on both teams are sure what the signal is, whether they recognize it or not. In the 1974 World Series between Oakland and the L.A. Dodgers, the A's Bert Campaneris came to bat with a runner on first. Bobby Winkles, the third-base coach, twice flashed Campaneris a sign, and both times Campaneris stepped out of the box. He obviously couldn't figure out the sign. Andy Messersmith, pitching for the Dodgers, lost patience. "Hey, he wants you to bunt!" shouted Messersmith. Campaneris nodded, bunted and moved the runner to second base.

Davey Johnson, manager of the New York Mets, recalled a game in 1985 when he gave the hit-and-run sign—an order to the runner on first to run on the pitch, and an order to the batter to swing and make contact, even on a bad pitch. The batter, Mookie Wilson, missed the sign and didn't swing. That should have hung the runner, Wally Backman, up to dry, but he missed the sign, too, and didn't run. Realizing his good fortune, Johnson gave up on the hit-and-run and signaled a bunt instead. This time Wilson and Backman caught the signal. The sacrifice worked, and Backman eventually scored the winning run.

Against San Diego the same season, the Mets fell victim to a surprise squeeze play, signaled in plain, spoken language by the Padres' third-base coach, Ozzie Virgil, to the batter, Carmelo Martinez. Trouble is, the language was Spanish—as foreign to most of the Mets' players as a sophisticated semaphore system. In Spanish, Virgil yelled, "Drop it down." Martinez laid down a perfect bunt, and Steve Garvey scored the winning run from third base.

The New York Giants used to use a different language. Luther "Dummy" Taylor, a Giant pitcher during the first decade of the 20th century,

Continued on page 34

With no chance to get Mickey Rivers at home on a squeeze play, Milwaukee catcher Charlie Moore—who has the play in front of him—tells the player fielding the bunt where to go for the out.

Signalmen

He's the manager's eyes and ears on the field, and the great communicator to batters and baserunners. He must know the tendencies of just about every player on the field, adding situational information for split-second decisions that can make the difference between winning and losing. "A good third base coach can win you several games a year," said Billy Martin. "He must think along with me, considering all the options and being ready for whatever I want to do." Third base coaches have two primary functions—giving signs and guiding runners. Good ones are also adept at stealing signs, but in giving signs a coach must make his motions clear enough so the batter and runner understand them, but not so clear that the opposition does. Most importantly, he must decide whether or not a runner should try and score, factoring in his runner's speed, the outfielder's arm strength, the score, how many are out, who's up next, what inning it is, how hard the wind is blowing, and whatever else he can think of.

Baltimore's Cal Ripken Sr. is the quintessential company man. With the Orioles since he broke into baseball in 1957, he's the perfect physical type for a third base coach: lean, angular and twitchy.

Good third base coaches give their signals to runners clearly and early. The Giants' Bill Fahey (left, 42) gives Kevin Mitchell the green light, while Seattle's Chuck Cottier (below, 15) gives the slide sign to Jack Perconte, and Bobby Knoop (above) gives a sign only his teammates can decipher.

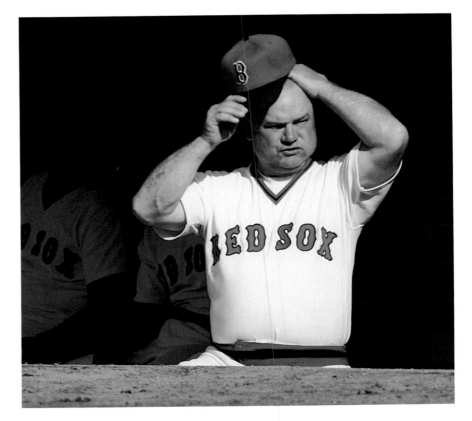

Don Zimmer's head has had a rough baseball career. A beaning in 1953 left him unconscious, and three years later a pitch fractured his cheekbone. But he used his noggin well in leading the 1989 Cubs to an unexpected NL East title, and also uses it to both think up and transmit signals.

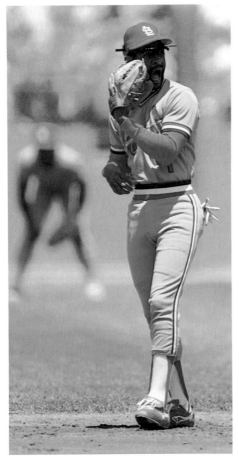

With defensive wizard Ozzie Smith at shortstop, second basemen were well-advised to keep their mouths shut and their ears open. Smith decided who would cover the bag.

was a deaf mute. John McGraw, the Giants' manager, ordered all his players to learn the sign language used by the deaf. McGraw used it as a backup signaling system. If a player didn't appear to understand McGraw's regular signal, he would get the player's attention and spell out "steal" or "bunt" with his fingers, in the sign language he had learned from Taylor.

Taylor wasn't the first deaf player to inspire a new signaling system. The flamboyant hand signals used by today's umpires for their calls—strike, ball, fair, foul, safe, out—were first used to help William "Dummy" Hoy, an outfielder who played for six big-league teams between 1888 and 1902.

When a player is traded to another team in the same league, his old team routinely changes its signals. But when the White Sox traded Zeke Bonura to the Washington Senators in 1938, Chicago manager Jimmy Dykes didn't bother. "Bonura never caught any of our signs when he played for us," Dykes reasoned. Bonura proved more observant than Dykes expected. In their first confrontation that season, the White Sox and Senators were tied, and Bonura—now a Senator—got to third base late in the game. In the Chicago dugout, Dykes absentmindedly touched his chin. The slow-footed Bonura took off for home, and so startled the Chicago pitcher that he threw wild, enabling Bonura to score the winning run. "I saw Dykes touch his chin and that's his sign to steal," Bonura explained. "I forgot I wasn't on his team anymore."

Slugger Frank Howard became a big-league manager in 1981, but when he was playing for the L.A. Dodgers in the early 1960s he sometimes had trouble catching signs. Preston Gomez, the Dodgers' third-base coach back then, recalled one such incident. "To help Frank, who had trouble

with signs, we told him that when we wanted him running with the pitch, our first-base coach, Pete Reiser, simply would shout Frank's last name," Gomez said. "So Frank got on base and Reiser yelled from the coaching box, 'Stay alive, Howard!' Frank didn't run. Before the next pitch, Reiser yelled again—only this time louder—'Stay alive, Howard!' Now Frank, kind of depressed, called Reiser to the bag and whispered, 'We've been friends for all these years, and I call you Pete. Why have you suddenly stopped calling me Frank?' "

Sometimes a player misses a sign on purpose. Chuck Connors gained fame as the star of a television series called *The Rifleman,* but he was a ballplayer first, with the Chicago Cubs in 1951. In a game against the Giants, Connors was sent up to pinch-hit against Sal Maglie; there were two men on, and the Cubs were trailing by two runs. The count went to three and one. Connors wasn't much of a hitter, and everyone knew that Cubs manager Phil Cavarretta would give him the "take" sign. Connors knew it, too, and reasoned that Maglie would throw a fastball down the middle. Connors recalled the situation this way: "I said to myself, 'You're barely hanging on with this club, and here you've got a chance to be a hero. Are you going to let this chance pass you by?' Well, the answer was no, so Maglie pitched, I swung, and hit one into the right-field seats. It felt great and I really took my time trotting around the bases, because I knew what was waiting for me. When I got back to the dugout, there was Cavarretta really glaring at me. I just looked at him and said, 'Don't holler. I know you're mad, and I'm probably on my way back to the minor leagues.' I was correct, because the next day I was gone—sent down for hitting a home run when I should have taken a pitch."

The signals a catcher uses to indicate the desired pitch don't vary much from team to team, but when a catcher the stature of Cincinnati's Johnny Bench (above) puts down two fingers for a curve, pitchers were well-advised not to shake him off.

5' 8" 155 lbs. b 5/14/37
BR TR d 6/17/87

DICK HOWSER
Manager

Although Dick Howser was one of the best-liked managers of the 1980s, his reputation as a nice guy belied his toughness. "When George [Steinbrenner] hired Dick Howser in 1979, he thought he was getting a nice, quiet little coach," said sportswriter Ed Linn. "Instead, he found himself with a tough little nut on his hands." When Steinbrenner made a suggestion, Howser listened, and then did it his own way; when Steinbrenner gave an order, Howser told Steinbrenner he was wrong, and then did it his own way. When Yankee stars Lou Piniella and Graig Nettles hit batting slumps in 1980, Howser used pinch hitters for them despite their protests. And Howser's way worked; the Yankees took the AL East division title.

Refusing to take orders from Steinbrenner got Howser fired by season's end, but he had been spotted by several other clubs and finally accepted an offer from the Royals. In Kansas City there was no doubt who was boss; Howser slipped easily into his managerial role and promptly led the Royals to the AL West title for the second half of the strike-torn 1981 season. Division titles followed in 1984 and in 1985, when the Royals went on to win the "War within the State" Series against St. Louis.

After managing the AL to an All-Star Game victory in 1986, Howser confronted an adversary even more stubborn than Steinbrenner or Whitey Herzog's Cardinals: a brain tumor. He battled the disease for nearly a year before he died in June 1987.

It's baseball's most basic—but also most important—sign, because not knowing how many outs there are can get you a quick trip to the minors. Catchers like Milwaukee's B.J. Surhoff (above) routinely help their teammates out.

Sometimes a situation calls for quick thinking on the part of a player, with no time for managerial initiative. In the 1952 World Series, Billy Martin, the Yankees' second baseman, used the brain for baseball that later made him a successful manager. The Dodgers were then managed by Chuck Dressen, who had managed Martin in the minor leagues. Brooklyn led the Series, two games to one. In the fifth inning of Game 4 the Dodgers trailed by a run, but got runners on second and third. Pitcher Joe Black came to bat and Dressen flashed him a sign—which Martin recognized as Dressen's squeeze sign from their minor league days. Martin flashed that information to catcher Yogi Berra, who called a pitchout—and easily tagged out the helpless runner who was trying to score from third.

Cardinal shortstop Marty Marion also made a heads-up play in the 1942 World Series against the Yankees in a pickoff situation involving Yankee baserunner Joe Gordon. A pickoff play can be initiated by a sign from the pitcher, the catcher or an infielder. Other times, the signal is simply a flash of daylight between the infielder and the runner—a space showing that the infielder is closer to the base than the runner. The Cardinals led the Series three games to one, and led Game 5, 4–2, going into the last of the ninth. The Yankees' Gordon, the MVP that year, singled, Bill Dickey got to first on an error, and with none out, Cardinal shortstop Marion saw a "daylight" pickoff opportunity.

"Jerry Priddy was the hitter," Marion recalled. "The bunt was in order. When you're defending on a bunt play, you play close to the runner to hold him on, and then you try to back off in a way so he thinks you're going to stay in position. You're trying to decoy the guy so he will take too big a lead. He wants to break far enough off second base so he can beat the throw to third on

a bunt, and he's very susceptible to a good pickoff. I had a knack of getting back of the runner pretty good."

Marion did, and catcher Walker Cooper saw daylight between his shortstop and Yankee runner Gordon. "Cooper came up throwing," Marion said. "I got behind Gordon and we had him good. We had him picked off *so far*. It wasn't a close play at all." The pickoff deflated the Yankee rally, and the Cardinals protected their lead and won the Series.

Phil Rizzuto, the great Yankee shortstop turned broadcaster, was a master at squeezing runners home from third. He'd call the squeeze himself from his position at the plate. Opposing players knew that and would try to catch the sign. "I'd first do something that would catch the runner's attention," Rizzuto explained. "One season, I'd turn to squawk at the umpire about a pitch he'd called a strike. That would catch the eye of the runner because I didn't often argue with umpires. Then, too, the opposing players wouldn't be watching me so closely, figuring I wouldn't give a sign while I was arguing. But I would. As I yelled at the umpire, I'd hold my left hand so the runner could see my palm. When I finished squawking, I'd peek at the runner. If he was holding his right hand so I could see his palm, I knew he'd gotten the sign and was answering. When I got the answer, the squeeze was on."

In 1951 the Yankees and Indians were tied for first place with 13 games to go. The two contenders took a 1–1 tie into the ninth inning, and Joe DiMaggio reached third, bringing up Rizzuto. Somehow, without the Indians catching it, Rizzuto flashed the suicide squeeze sign to DiMaggio. Rizzuto dropped a perfect bunt, DiMaggio scored the winning run, and Bob Lemon, the Cleveland pitcher, angrily threw his glove and the ball into the stands. The Yanks held on to win their third straight pennant.

When everyone gets the sign, the hit-and-run can be one of baseball's prettiest plays. The runner on first breaks for second, the second baseman goes to cover the bag, and the batter slaps a hit through the resulting vacancy. Here, the Giants' Jose Uribe does the hitting, Robby Thompson the running.

Zack Taylor took a manager's holiday on August 24, 1951, as St. Louis Browns owner Bill Veeck decided to let the fans make all the game decisions against the Philadelphia Athletics. Circuit Court Judge James E. McLaughlin estimated the votes, then relayed the decision to coach John Berardino. The Browns won, 5-3, one of just 52 wins all season.

For all the brilliance and skullduggery of managers and players, fans often think they could make out a better lineup and call plays at least as well as the uniformed incumbents. When Bill Veeck owned the pitiful St. Louis Browns in 1951, he gave fans their chance, designating the fans seated in the section behind the Browns' dugout "grandstand managers" and giving each of them "YES" and "NO" placards. Zack Taylor, the Browns' manager, was seated in a rocking chair on top of the dugout. He wore slippers and smoked a pipe. The visiting Philadelphia Athletics scored three runs in the first inning and had runners on first and third. "SHALL WE WARM UP PITCHER?" the fans were asked. "NO," they replied, keeping faith with Ned Garver, the Browns' starter and the team's only real star. "INFIELD BACK?" "YES," voted the fans, and Pete Suder grounded into a double play. Garver settled down and the Browns won, 5–3, with key hits contributed by Sherm Lollar and Hank "Bow Wow" Arft, benchwarmers whom the fans had voted into the starting lineup.

As Detroit's Sparky Anderson says, "You don't have to be a Harvard professor to manage baseball." But Veeck's stunt and Anderson's modesty play on the fans' thirst to participate, at least vicariously, in the strategy of the game and the signaling that sets it in motion. Baseball is, in fact, a complex game, a mixture of athletic skills and mental strategies. The third-base coach may look kind of funny out there, but he's molding skills into strategy —and giving us much of the game we love so well. ◗I

When signals get crossed, baseball can become a hazardous game. Although the ball got away as Cincinnati superstar Eric Davis (44) collided with teammates Luis Quinones (10) and Rolando Roomes (36), the players escaped unharmed.

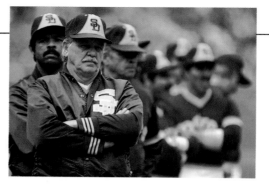

Dick Williams

Popularity was never Dick Williams' strong suit. Winning was. Oh, he could be one of the guys if he wanted to, like when he was hired to manage the wild and woolly Oakland A's in 1971 and abandoned his crewcut in favor of long hair and a mustache. But most of the time Williams' strict discipline, sharp tongue and old school methods made him a loner in his own dugout. He didn't really care if his players liked him or not. All he asked was that they respect his knowledge of the game and do things his way. He had a very simple, straightforward slant on the player-manager relationship. "You don't have to go out to dinner with these guys," he said. "Just put the names of the best players in the lineup. If they do the job, they play. If they don't, they don't. And don't be afraid to tell anyone if he screwed up."

Whatever he did, it worked. In an age when managers got fired as often as summer barbecues, Williams was a true survivor, lasting 21 years and winning four pennants, two world championships and three Manager of the Year awards. He is one of only two managers in history—Bill McKechnie is the other—to win pennants with three different teams.

But if it hadn't been for one bad landing, Williams might have made his name as a player instead of a manager. A three-sport star in high school, Williams was signed by Brooklyn in 1947 and played in the talent-rich Dodger farm system until 1951, when he was promoted to the majors. He was on the verge of gaining a permanent spot in the Dodger outfield in 1952 when, in a game against St. Louis, he dived for a ball and suffered a severe shoulder separation. With his throwing arm permanently weakened by the injury, Williams became a utility player, spending much of his career with the lowly Baltimore Orioles and Kansas City Athletics.

As with many future managers, Williams used his time on the bench well. And he was lucky. He learned the game first as a player in the Dodger organization, where baseball was also a classroom sport. Designed and run by Branch Rickey, the Dodger system was a managerial factory, turning out the likes of Eddie Stanky, Leo Durocher, Walter Alston, Gene Mauch, Gil Hodges, Bobby Bragan and Danny Ozark. "We'd have to keep notebooks and be tested," Williams said. "We had lectures at night—George Sisler on hitting, Pepper Martin on sliding. And you had to remember what they had to say." Williams also became a premier bench jockey. "Mostly I'd sit there on the bench and heckle the bleep out of the other club," he said.

The rest of Williams' managerial apprenticeship was served as a player under Oriole skipper Paul Richards, another of the game's great teachers. Richards played Williams all over the infield and outfield, giving him a thorough understanding of how each position should be played. "Williams is my type of athlete," Richards said, "one of those fellows who isn't afraid of winning."

Williams wound up his 13-year playing career with Boston in 1964, then was offered the managing job at Toronto, the Red Sox' top minor league team. While the Red Sox finished ninth in 1965 and 1966, Williams led Toronto to back-to-back championships. In 1967 he got the job he wanted—manager of the Red Sox—but he inherited a team that was weakest in the areas that Williams prized most: pitching and defense. In addition, the Red Sox were undisci-

To last 21 years as a major league manager a man has to be flexible. Dick Williams shifted his philosophy to fit each of the six teams he managed. "I never play by the book," he said, "because I never met the guy who wrote it."

plined, sloppy and unfocused. Williams quickly gave them a reason to unite—a common enemy, namely the manager. He drove the team hard in spring training, emphasizing fundamentals. Stern physical conditioning, curfews and bed checks replaced the country club atmosphere of the year before, and Williams boldly predicted that "this team will win more than it will lose this season."

Boston came within one game of a world title in 1967, and Williams was named Manager of the Year. "I had no friends on that team," he said. "I was sarcastic and belligerent, but I got the most out of the players." Two years later Williams became the scapegoat as the Red Sox sank to third in the AL East, and he was fired. He spent one season as a coach under Gene Mauch in Montreal, calling the season "a clinic in inside baseball."

In 1971 Oakland owner Charlie Finley came calling, and Williams inherited a talented, boisterous, mustachioed bunch of A's. The A's already had a common enemy in Finley, so Williams could be one of the boys. "When I managed the Red Sox, I had a butch haircut; with Oakland I was as hairy as the rest of them," he said. "Times change, I had to change with them."

What didn't change was Williams' ability to bring home a winner. The A's won three straight AL West titles and back-to-back world titles in 1972 and 1973. But Williams was also a man of principle, and when Finley tried to get second baseman Mike Andrews to sign a statement proclaiming himself unfit to play after Andrews committed two errors in a World Series game, Williams had had enough. He announced he would resign at the end of the Series. "The Andrews

Williams (left) called the A's 3-2 win over Cincinnati in Game 7 of the 1972 World Series his "biggest thrill in baseball ever." But it didn't come easy. Williams came out of the dugout about 60 times during the Series, and took 38 trips to the mound. He even coached first base in key situations.

thing was the last straw," he said. "It was all off after that. My players were unhappy and I was caught in the middle." A's catcher Gene Tenace said "Dick Williams left for the players."

Williams signed with the California Angels in 1974 as baseball's first $100,000 manager, but foundered. He spent five years at the helm in Montreal, helping to turn the expansion Expos into perennial contenders, then headed west to San Diego. In 1984 he had his last championship season as the Padres —who had never finished higher than fourth—won the NL pennant. It was a classic Williams team: young, hard-working and fundamentally sound. "Williams has to be given credit for turning the Padres around," general manager Jack McKeon said. "He made them believe they could win."

And as tough as Williams could be on players, his sense of fairness was unassailable. "I'll give him

this—he gets on everyone the same; the stars get it the way the extra men get it," said Padre third baseman Graig Nettles.

Williams' gruff style may have obscured his ability as a strategist. He made sure that his teams were prepared to gain an edge whenever the opportunity for one arose. "There are no real secrets in this game," he said. "The edges are very few, but they are there and you have to know how to take advantage of them."

Even though he was far from the game's most popular manager, few players complained at the end of the season. "I've never had a player hate me so much that he refused his postseason check," Williams said. He never set out to be liked. He set out to win. "I'll take all the criticism there is if we win the World Series. Criticism doesn't bother me. Only losing does."

DICK
WILLIAMS

Manager
Boston Red Sox 1967-1969
Oakland Athletics 1971-1973
California Angels 1974-1976
Montreal Expos 1977-1981
San Diego Padres 1982-1985
Seattle Mariners 1986-1988

GAMES	3,023
WINS	
Career	1,571
Season High	101
LOSSES	
Career	1,451
Season High	89
WINNING PERCENTAGE	
Career	.520
Season High	.627
DIVISION TITLES	1971, 1972, 1973, 1984
PENNANTS	1967, 1972, 1973, 1984
WORLD CHAMPIONSHIPS	1972, 1973

In 1981 Williams was reminded that managers are only as good as their team's last game. He'd taken the Expos from the NL East cellar to consecutive second-place finishes in 1979 and 1980, then was fired in September 1981 with his club just one game out of first.

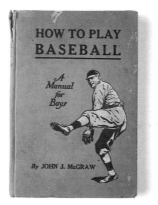

HOW TO PLAY
BASEBALL

A Manual for Boys

By JOHN J. McGRAW

Scientific Baseball

Back in 1891 the Baltimore Orioles—"the old Orioles," as they came to be called—picked up an 18-year-old infielder who stood only 5′ 7″ and weighed 121 pounds. In 1892 they took on a manager whose teams had never finished higher than fifth. In 1893 they traded for a shortstop who was batting .136, and in an 1894 trade they got an outfielder who was only 5′ 4½″ tall. It doesn't sound like much now and it didn't then, but as things turned out, those old Orioles changed the face of baseball. The players were John McGraw, Hughie Jennings and Willie Keeler; the manager was Ned Hanlon. Together, they won three National League pennants and developed many of the strategies used in baseball today. McGraw and Jennings refined those strategies during successful managerial careers of their own. The strategies of the old Orioles came to be known as "inside baseball." Devotees so admired—and exaggerated—the precision of teams managed by Hanlon and McGraw that they came up with yet another name: "scientific baseball."

The elements of scientific baseball—the bunt, the hit-and-run and run-and-hit, the stolen base and double steal—are still in use. Hitters are taught to foul off pitches, to bunt, to hit behind the runner and to go the other way with an outside pitch; pitchers learn to mix pitches, change speeds and keep baserunners close; fielders practice defenses for every conceivable situation. The innovations of Hanlon and McGraw, polished by other managers and altered to fit the changing conditions of play, are now called base-

In John McGraw's day, "scientific baseball" denoted a style of play. Today it also means using technology. Milwaukee batting coach Don Baylor (opposite) uses videotape to help analyze the swing of Brewer infielder Bill Spiers.

Nothing that happened on a ballfield escaped the withering gaze of New York Giants manager John McGraw (second from right). McGraw was especially intent on winning the 1917 World Series, as his Giants had lost their last three Series. But the Giants were beaten again in six games by the Chicago White Sox, managed by Pants Rowland (above, center).

ball's "fundamentals." By any name, the totality of scientific baseball is greater than the sum of its parts, because in essence it means outsmarting your opponent, tailoring your strategy to use every bit of talent on your roster and doing every little thing that might score—or prevent—another run. "Everybody knows all the strategies," Earl Weaver once said. "Nothing's changed in a hundred years. A manager's job is to select the best players for what he wants done."

A hundred years ago, however, baseball was changing very rapidly, and new strategies were being tested all the time. In 1866 Dickey Pearce of the Brooklyn Atlantics laid down the first bunt. He reached first base safely, but his innovation was scorned as a "baby hit." To avoid a tag, runners used to run *around* the base and try to touch it from the back; then Mike "King" Kelly of the 1880s White Stockings developed the "Chicago slide," the original hook slide. In the beginning, the curveball was illegal; the spitball was legal; pitchers threw from only 45 feet away, but were not allowed to bend their elbows; bats could be flat on one side; and foul balls didn't count as strikes.

In the championship series of 1885 and 1886, the Chicago White Stockings of the National League faced the St. Louis Browns of the American Association—a major league back then. The Browns played their infield back and had their pitcher cover first base on ground balls hit to his left. "The fielding of the pitchers of the St. Louis team was an innovation in baseball, and their covering of first base at a dead run, and backing up on plays was wonderful," wrote John J. Evers and Hugh S. Fullerton in 1910. "They enabled [Charles] Comiskey to play a deep first base and he, playing deep, gave the

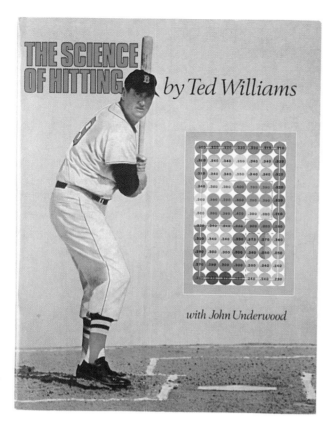

THE SCIENCE OF HITTING *by Ted Williams*

with *John Underwood*

Ted Williams took the science of hitting to unprecedented levels, even so far as to dissect the strike zone and insert what average he'd hit for, based on where pitches crossed the plate. The batter's box was his laboratory, and he put in long hours. "No one has come up with a substitute for hard work," he said.

second baseman a chance to play deeper and closer to the base, which helped the shortstop by many feet."

The White Stockings' infield strategy sounds elementary, hardly worth the praise of Evers, who was a star second baseman for the Chicago Cubs, and Fullerton, a veteran and pioneering sportswriter. But in the late 19th century all these plays and strategies had to be thought out and tested—and often revised—to fit frequent changes in baseball rules. When something worked, it was quickly copied by other teams. Good plays were sifted through the mesh of experience and were combined with others to form strategies. And the team that did more sifting than any other was the old Orioles, and the manager who carried the process forward during the first three decades of the 20th century was John McGraw.

Even as a rookie, McGraw, a left-handed hitter, impressed Hanlon with his ability to hit to left field, a rare skill back then. "Nobody is a real hitter unless he can hit to all fields," McGraw told Hanlon, who quickly agreed. McGraw had only a grammar-school education, but his energy and ambition led him to spend his off-seasons taking courses at St. Bonaventure College in New York state. In exchange for tuition, room and board, he coached the baseball team, herding the players into a cold basement in January and drilling them on fundamentals, some of which were new even in the major leagues.

Third baseman McGraw and shortstop Hughie Jennings became close friends—both loved to talk baseball by the hour—and after the 1893 season Jennings joined McGraw at St. Bonaventure, giving the school's baseball team two major league coaches. At 20, McGraw was younger than some of

Pittsburgh's Max Carey was a self-made .300 hitter. After a disastrous rookie season in the minors, he taught himself to switch-hit, choked up on the bat and wound up with six .300 seasons, 738 stolen bases and a plaque in Cooperstown.

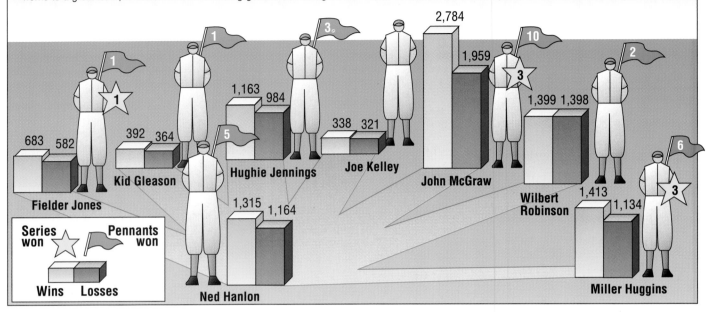

The Manager Maker

Ned Hanlon's Orioles won three consecutive NL pennants from 1894 to 1896. Their reputation as some of the savviest — and dirtiest — players in history survives to this day. But Orioles Park was not just home to a great team, it was a veritable breeding ground for managers who relied on Hanlon's inside baseball to dominate the game through the dead-ball era and beyond. Later with Brooklyn and Cincinnati, Hanlon trained future managers Fielder Jones and Miller Huggins. Hanlon's record includes five pennants and a .530 winning percentage.

Fielder Jones — 683 / 582 — 1
Kid Gleason — 392 / 364 — 1
Hughie Jennings — 1,163 / 984 — 3
Joe Kelley — 338 / 321
John McGraw — 2,784 / 1,959 — 10 / 3
Ned Hanlon — 1,315 / 1,164 — 5
Wilbert Robinson — 1,399 / 1,398 — 2
Miller Huggins — 1,413 / 1,134 — 6 / 3

Series won (star) — Pennants won (flag)
Wins   Losses

the students. Jennings, 24, wasn't much older. But both men knew the game and had the presence to command.

Like all successful managers, McGraw also had an *eye* for baseball. He knew talent when he saw it, he recognized flaws and he knew how to correct them. Jennings hit .182 in 1893, and McGraw saw why. Instead of stepping toward the pitcher as he swung, the right-handed Jennings stepped partly toward third base. In baseball jargon, he "stepped in the bucket." McGraw drilled that bad habit out of Jennings during their college practices, and by 1894 Jennings' average climbed to .335. And it kept climbing: to .386 in 1895 and to .398 in 1896.

The Orioles won pennants all three of those seasons, and Keeler hit as well as Jennings—.371, .391, .392, leading up to an amazing .424 in 1897, when the Orioles slipped to second place. McGraw batted .340, .369 and .325 in those Baltimore pennant seasons. The hitters had a big edge, because foul balls didn't count as strikes unless the umpire thought the batter was hitting fouls on purpose. McGraw learned to slash hard fouls—too hard for an ump to call intentional. If he got a good pitch, he would go for a hit; otherwise he tried to keep hitting fouls until he coaxed a walk. "He simply worries the life out of you," said Clark Griffith, an ace pitcher for Chicago. Leading off in the Oriole batting order, McGraw got to first base nearly half the time. Keeler batted second and, as he described his own success, he "hit 'em where they ain't." Faking a steal of second to find out whether the second baseman or shortstop was covering, McGraw then flashed the hit-and-run sign to Keeler. McGraw took off on the next pitch, and as the infielder moved to cover second, Keeler slapped the ball through the vacated hole, McGraw taking third on the single. The Orioles

Kirk Gibson can beat opponents with power, grit or speed. An All-American wide receiver in college, Gibson averaged 27 home runs and 30 stolen bases a season from 1984 to 1988.

didn't invent the hit-and-run, but they were the first team to make it the fulcrum of a winning strategy.

Until 1893 the pitcher worked only 50 feet from home plate. The present distance of 60 feet 6 inches was established in 1893, and Hanlon soon seized the strategic advantage. Bunts took longer to field, so Hanlon had his players practice bunting by the hour, using the bunt both as a sacrifice and as a way to get on base. Hanlon's swift runners also learned to slash down on the ball, chopping it into the hard ground in front of the plate. The high bounce often allowed the hitter time to reach first; the ploy became known as the "Baltimore chop."

On defense, the Orioles developed plays to counter double-steal attempts. With runners on first and third, the second baseman or shortstop moved to a cutoff position behind the mound. The runner on first was sure to attempt stealing second, but if the runner on third took off for home, the cutoff man could intercept the catcher's throw and throw home; if the runner stayed on third, he let the catcher's throw go through to second base. Wilbert Robinson, the Oriole catcher and another leader of Hanlon's "scientific" team, also developed the "sucker throw"—a full-arm fake throw to second, followed by a quick throw to McGraw at third to trap the lead runner.

The Orioles finished eighth in 1893. In 1894 their new strategic dash dumbfounded their opponents. They swept four games from the Giants to open the season, and the New York manager, John Montgomery Ward, expressed outrage at the slash-and-run Oriole tactics. "That's trick stuff by a lot of kids," he huffed. "I'm not sure what they're doing is legal." It was, and it worked; McGraw and Keeler pulled off 13 successful

Continued on page 52

Perhaps the most famous number-two hitter in history, Baltimore's Willie Keeler slapped hits through holes in the infield created by the aggressive baserunning of leadoff hitter John McGraw. Keeler averaged 220 hits a season in his five years with the Orioles, and his philosophy was simple: "Keep your eye clear and hit 'em where they ain't."

Home of the Angels

Anaheim Stadium

Anaheim Stadium

Baseball in Anaheim, California—freeway capital of the free world—got off to a predictable start. When Anaheim Stadium opened on April 19, 1966, a water main broke on one of the city's main streets, and the resulting traffic jam delayed fans and caused the game to start 20 minutes late.

The Angels lost their home opener, 3–1, to the White Sox, but the game marked the end of the team's nomadic early history. After spending 1961, their rookie season, in Los Angeles' tiny Wrigley Field, and then sharing space at Dodger Stadium for four years, the Los Angeles Angels moved 25 miles southeast to Anaheim. The stadium went up on schedule, with room for 43,250 fans, 12,000 cars and 200 buses. Its most distinguishing feature was an A-frame scoreboard 230 feet high—giving the stadium its nickname, the Big A—topped with a giant halo. And the California Angels were born.

The team finished sixth in its first season in Anaheim, but attendance skyrocketed to 1.4 million, more than twice the previous year's draw. For its first 14 seasons the stadium was a pitcher's park, as its lack of outfield stands provided both a poor background for hitters and a wind that generally blew in toward the plate. The 1967 All-Star Game featured just 17 hits and 30 strikeouts in the NL's 15-inning, 2–1 win. In 1972 Nolan Ryan arrived and Anaheim Stadium became the strikeout capital of the majors. Ryan won seven strikeout titles in the next eight seasons, and teammate Frank Tanana won the only one Ryan didn't. Ryan also tossed two no-hitters there.

The team won no titles until 1979, when manager Jim Fregosi—an Angel shortstop for their first 11 years—and league MVP Don Baylor led the Angels to the top of the AL West, although they lost the ALCS in four to Baltimore. In 1982 the Angels won another title and another chance. Facing Milwaukee in the ALCS, the Angels took a 2–0 lead at home but dropped the next three games on the road, becoming the first team ever to squander a 2–0 lead in a best-of-five championship series. The Angels won their third division title in 1986 but again suffered a heartbreaking loss in the ALCS. In Game 5 the Angels were one strike away from giving manager Gene Mauch his first World Series appearance in 25 years in the majors when Boston's Dave Henderson homered in the ninth to keep the Red Sox alive. Boston went on to win the game in 11 innings, then swept past the Angels in Games 6 and 7—at Fenway Park.

Despite the postseason disappointments, the Angels have been a big hit ever since their first title in 1979. In 1980 the addition of outfield stands raised the stadium's capacity to 65,158 and took away the pitcher's advantage. The Big A soon became the site of some historic hitting exploits, including Reggie Jackson's 500th career homer in 1984 and Rod Carew's 3,000th career hit in 1985.

With a consistently powerful lineup—and 26 entrance lanes and 28 exit lanes making traffic jams a thing of the past—the Angels drew at least two million fans every year in the 1980s, except the strike-shortened 1981 season. But on Opening Day 1990, the pitchers regained control, at least temporarily, as California's Mark Langston combined with Mike Witt to no-hit Seattle, giving Anaheim Stadium its sixth no-hitter.

Where once alfalfa, corn and oranges grew, now stands Anaheim Stadium, built in 1966 in Orange County, California, a few miles from Disneyland. The stadium cost $24 million to build.

Anaheim Stadium

2000 State College Boulevard
Anaheim, California

Built 1966

California Angels, AL
  1966-present

Seating Capacity
65,158

Style
Superstructure with
natural surface

Height of Outfield Fences
8 feet

Dugouts
Home: 3rd base
Visitor: 1st base

Bullpens
Home: right field
Visitor: left field

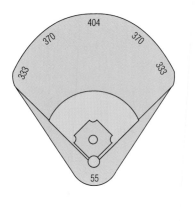

John McGraw would have loved Nellie Fox (right). Fox was a fine bunter, an outstanding defensive second baseman and an all-around hard-nosed guy. He led the White Sox to a pennant in 1959, played in 798 consecutive games during his career and struck out an average of just once every 43 at-bats, third best on the all-time list.

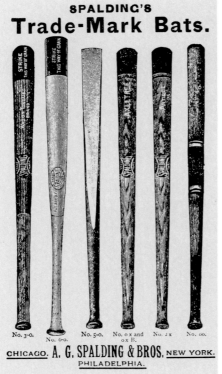

From 1885 to 1893, bats that were flat on one side were legal in the National League. They were especially handy for bunting and slap hitting, two potent offensive weapons for John McGraw and his Oriole teammates.

hit-and-runs before someone stopped them. But McGraw and his teammates also cheated outrageously. They sharpened their spikes, deliberately spiked opposing players, cut across the diamond from first to third when the ump wasn't looking and pioneered the art of dishonest groundskeeping. In addition to building up the baselines so that bunts would stay fair, the Oriole groundskeeper mixed soap chips into the dirt on the mound. The opposing pitcher's hand would get slippery, and his pitches would get wild; Oriole pitchers knew where to find pure dirt.

John Heydler, an NL umpire in the 1890s and later president of the National League, said: "We hear a lot of the glories of the old Orioles. Yes, they were a great team: they could run, hit, steal bases, and introduced a lot of fine plays into baseball. But there is another side of the picture which seldom is told today. The Orioles were mean, vicious, ready at any time to maim a rival player or an umpire, if it helped their cause. The things they would say to an umpire were unbelievably vile, and they broke the spirits of some fine men. I've seen umpires bathe their feet by the hour after McGraw and others spiked them through their shoes. The worst of it was that they got away with much of their browbeating and hooliganism. Seeing them unpunished for flagrant misconduct on the field, other clubs patterned after them, and I feel the lot of the umpire never was worse than in the years that the Orioles were flying high."

Heydler's views were widely shared. When the American League attained major league status in 1901, its president, Ban Johnson, emphasized respect for umpires and dealt sternly with abusive players. The Baltimore franchise moved to the new league with McGraw as manager—Hanlon had taken his managing skills to Brooklyn, where he won two more

pennants—and McGraw quickly ran afoul of Johnson's civilizing rules. In July 1902 Johnson suspended McGraw indefinitely. So McGraw jumped back to the old rough-and-tumble NL as manager of the New York Giants. He managed the Giants until June 3, 1932, winning ten pennants and three world championships.

McGraw was a tyrant but a great manager, and his strategic concepts were copied throughout baseball. Although often genial off the field, in uniform he continued to be vulgar and combative; to him, winning was everything. He inspired fierce loyalty from many of his players, though his interest in them was defined entirely by their ability to help the Giants win. McGraw so admired the pitching skill of Chicago's Mordecai "Three Finger" Brown that he considered having a digit or two amputated from the hands of his own pitchers. He was dissuaded only when told that Brown's skill did not result from his shortage of fingers.

McGraw was 29 when he took over the Giants. He believed he knew more about baseball than anyone else in the game—and he was probably right. He and Hanlon had already changed the game from one depending on slugging to one emphasizing speed, deception and synchronized teamwork.

McGraw didn't keep the detailed data on every player that Earl Weaver did, nor did he have the computerized information used by Tony LaRussa. But he kept an amazing amount of information in his head, and he used it constantly. In an instructional book that he wrote in 1913, McGraw said: "Baseball is largely a matter of chance and probability, and it is the man who can figure the chances closest and get the right answer the greatest number of times who is the best leader."

In addition to being one of the finest defensive shortstops in major league history, Larry Bowa (left) was also a major pain to opponents, umpires and eventually his own players. Bowa was hired to manage San Diego in 1987, but his temper tantrums helped to get him fired early in 1988 after a career 81–127 mark.

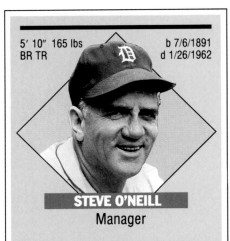

5' 10" 165 lbs
BR TR
b 7/6/1891
d 1/26/1962

STEVE O'NEILL
Manager

Some fans thought Steve O'Neill was way too relaxed: he didn't rail at players; he didn't lose his temper when things went wrong. When his 1937 Indians dropped from first place, the *Cleveland News* ran the headline: "Get Mad, Steve." But he couldn't. As a man who had worked in the coal mines, he took a philosophical view of the game: "I thank my stars for baseball every day of my life," O'Neill said. "It got me and most of my brothers out of the mines."

O'Neill signed on with the Indians in 1911, and from 1915 to 1925 he was known as the smartest catcher in baseball. He was so skilled at handling pitchers that he lasted 17 years in the majors, despite some weak seasons at bat.

As a manager, O'Neill was just as sharp: over 14 years at the helm of four major league teams, he never had a losing season. His first job came in 1935, when he took the helm for his old Cleveland team in midseason. The Indians had played .489 that year until O'Neill arrived; under him, they played .610. The next season, O'Neill brought 17-year-old Bob Feller up from the minors. And to give the young pitcher the benefit of experience, O'Neill got behind the plate himself.

When the Indians finished fourth in 1937, O'Neill was fired. But six years later he was back in the majors, and there his easygoing style served him well: he led the Tigers to a world championship in 1945.

Fouling off pitches was a specialty of John McGraw, but Rabbit Maranville (above) once won a game by fouling off 16 pitches in a row. The delay took the game past a 6:30 p.m. curfew and erased the lead the opposition had taken in the top of the inning.

McGraw thrived on the tactics of the dead-ball era, because they made baseball more of a chess game; since relatively few games were decided by home runs, it made sense to play for one run at a time. Other managers took pages from McGraw's book, and as the hit-and-run and other such plays became standard, the idea of individual heroics paled. Evers, the Cub second baseman, and Fullerton, the sportswriter, titled their 1910 book *Touching Second: The Science of Baseball,* and had this to say: "The game has developed toward exact science steadily for the last fifteen years. If there is a serious menace to the popularity of the national game it is that the playing will become mechanical, if not monotonous."

That was an exaggeration, but the Giants certainly thrived on McGraw's disciplined system. His great managing rival was Connie Mack of the Philadelphia Athletics, who had as great an eye for talent as McGraw, but tended to let his players take the initiative. Between 1902 and 1914, Mack's Athletics won six pennants while McGraw's Giants won five. They played head-to-head in three World Series—1905, 1911 and 1913—and the A's won two of the three. After Mack's 1914 pennant, however, he sold off his stars and the A's dropped into last place for seven straight years. McGraw's Giants continued to contend, winning the pennant in 1917, finishing second for three straight seasons, then winning four straight pennants starting in 1921.

Even before that pennant string, McGraw clearly considered himself the winner in his rivalry with Mack. Moreover, he knew the reason why, and expressed his philosophy in an article for the May 1920 issue of *Baseball Magazine.* "Connie's system, in a nut shell, is to build up a team that runs itself," McGraw wrote. "My system, in a nut shell, is to build up a team that I can run."

Run it he did. Burleigh Grimes, a Hall of Famer who pitched for the Giants and five other NL teams during a 19-year career, described McGraw's approach: "If you'd made a bad play he'd say, 'Son, come over here and sit down by me.' You'd do that and he would say, 'Now, why did you make that play that way?' Usually the fellow would say, 'I thought—' and McGraw would interrupt and say, 'What with? You just do the playing. I'll do the thinking for this club.' "

Although McGraw had helped to invent scientific baseball, he wasn't reluctant to turn his back on it occasionally for the sake of surprise. "McGraw, more than any other manager who I ever saw or heard about, wasn't afraid of taking on responsibility," said Grimes. "McGraw's was an aggressive game. He was a slasher. He'd run on you, play hit-and-run, suck you in for the bunt and then hit by you. He liked those guys who'd hustle and break their necks to win a game, like [Frankie] Frisch and Ross Youngs —guys who could do the unexpected and get away with it, who were daring, daring but never reckless."

Hughie Jennings, McGraw's old Baltimore teammate, carried his skills to Detroit, where he managed the Tigers to pennants in 1907, 1908 and 1909. Like Hanlon but unlike McGraw, Jennings didn't mind letting players use their brains—particularly smart players like Ty Cobb, who starred for the Detroit champions. Cobb practiced his "scientific baseball" on the field, with help from teammates like "Wahoo Sam" Crawford, a superb hitter in his own right who nevertheless played in Cobb's shadow. "Talk about strategy and playing with your head, that was Cobb all the way," Crawford said. "A lot of times Cobb would be on third base and I'd draw

When you've got the extra-base power of a Don Mattingly, you can almost always get a bunt hit if you really need to. Mattingly has outstanding bat control—in his first eight seasons in the majors he had just 238 strikeouts to go along with 164 home runs.

One of McGraw's favorite players was shortstop Travis "Stonewall" Jackson (above, at bat). In addition to his great fielding and solid bat, Jackson was as tough as they came. He once played an entire season on a pair of injured knees that, according to fellow NL shortstop Dick Bartell, "wouldn't support a pregnant sparrow."

a base on balls, and as I started to go down to first I'd sort of half glance at Cobb, at third. He'd make a slight move that told me he wanted me to keep going—not to stop at first, but to keep on going to second. Well, I'd trot two-thirds of the way to first and then suddenly, without warning, I'd speed up and go across first as fast as I could and tear out for second. He's on third, see. They're watching him, and suddenly there I go, and they don't know what the devil to do. If they try to stop me, Cobb'll take off for home. Sometimes they'd catch him, and sometimes they'd catch me, and sometimes they wouldn't get either of us. But most of the time they were too paralyzed to do anything, and I'd wind up at second on a base on balls."

Jimmy McAleer, a rival AL manager, called Cobb "the greatest piece of baseball machinery that ever stepped on the diamond." Cobb's statistics dazzle us today: a .367 lifetime batting average covering 24 seasons; 12 AL batting championships, nine of them in a row from 1907 through 1915; six stolen-base championships; and 892 stolen bases in all. In his day, however, Cobb was praised as much for his head as for his physical skill. In 1910 Charles Comiskey, a pioneering player and manager who by then owned the Chicago White Sox, pronounced Cobb "the greatest player of all time." Cobb, Comiskey said, "plays ball with his whole anatomy—his head, his arms, his hands, his legs, his feet."

In modern parlance, Cobb psyched out opposing players. Although it is now considered rude—"bush"—to steal bases and pile on runs after your team is safely ahead, Cobb considered it good strategy. "If we cannot only beat them, but run wild on them in addition, treat them like a lot of bush leaguers, it is liable to put them up in the air for a week," he said. His goal, he said, was "a general demoralization of the opposition."

obb managed the Tigers from 1921 through 1926. Both he and McGraw were managing as Babe Ruth brought the home run into baseball, changing strategy for all time. McGraw and Cobb hated it; they thought the game they loved and had so largely developed might be gone for good. "The time is here," Cobb wrote longingly in his 1961 autobiography, "for a return to the old game of hit-and-run, the steal and double steal, the bunt in all its wonderful varieties, the squeeze, the ball hit to the opposite field and the ball punched through openings in the defense for a single."

In fact, scientific baseball was *not* dead, though for years it appeared to be, particularly during the 1950s, when virtually every team built its offense entirely around power hitting. Then, however, better pitching, better defense and bigger ballparks revived the running game. No one calls it "scientific baseball" any more, but the plays developed by McGraw and dramatized by Cobb are much in use today. If McGraw liked to direct his players almost like puppets, he should see today's teams, with coaches instructing players on the minute details of the game, and managers changing pitchers with a frequency unknown in the old days. Baseball was never a science. It is a game of athletic skill and teamwork, intelligently applied—as it was in the old days by Ned Hanlon, John McGraw, Ty Cobb and other pioneers of "scientific baseball." 🔘

Yankee shortstop Phil Rizzuto (above, throwing) was a decent hitter, but he made his fortune with his glove. "My best pitch," said Yankee right-hander Vic Raschi, "is anything the batter grounds, lines or pops in the direction of Rizzuto."

Hughie Jennings

Hughie Jennings had a soft heart but a hard head. His skull—which housed a fine strategic mind—was fractured three times: once by a fastball from Amos Rusie, "the Hoosier Thunderbolt," once by an ill-advised dive into an empty swimming pool and once when Jennings' car went off the side of a mountain.

His career as a major league player and manager was only slightly less tumultuous. He played shortstop for the three-time NL champion Baltimore Orioles in the late 1890s and took a back seat only to teammate John McGraw when it came to annoying and harassing the opposition. He managed a talented but strife-torn Detroit club to three pennants, this time in the AL, all the while turning the third-base coach's box into his own personal theater. And he ended his career back with McGraw as they brought their old Oriole style of play to the New York Giants and won four straight pennants in the 1920s.

But Jennings was no McGraw clone. He allowed the game to be fun and was much more sympathetic to his players than his hard-bitten colleague McGraw. Jennings was among the first managers to take different motivational approaches to their players depending on the players' temperaments, and nowhere was this flexibility more warranted—or more crucial—than with Ty Cobb. Jennings disliked Cobb, as did virtually all of Cobb's teammates, but he recognized his talent and made special accommodations for it. He excused Cobb from team practices and generally left him alone. "There is nothing I can teach Cobb," he said. "I might only rob him of the gift God gave him. Cobb can be the greatest player of all time if allowed to go his own way." Cobb went on to win batting titles in each of Jennings' first nine years as manager.

Jennings' baseball career got its start—like so many others of its time—in the coal mines of Pennsylvania. He left school at the age of 12 to work in the mines for 90 cents a day but wound up playing semi-pro ball for $5 a game. He won a battle with tuberculosis at 15 and made the majors with Louisville in 1891. In July 1893 he was sold to Baltimore, where he spent most of the season nursing a sore arm and learning about the game from manager Ned Hanlon. Over the next three years—all championship seasons for Baltimore—Jennings hit .335, .386 and .401, and stole a total of 160 bases. Hanlon's Orioles would do anything to get on base, and Jennings' specialty was getting hit by a pitch, which he did 49 times in 1896. He was brilliant in the field as well and was the model for Hall of Famer Honus Wagner's defensive play. "Jennings was the first shortstop never to leave his position until the hitter either hit the ball or missed it," Wagner said. "He had wonderful reflexes."

He also had a law degree, earned in exchange for coaching the Cornell University baseball team. After suffering another arm injury in 1900, Jennings hung up his spikes and hung out his shingle. But he was back in baseball a year later, and after a stint as player-manager of a minor league team, he was hired in 1907 by owner Frank Navin to manage the Tigers.

Jennings persuaded the Tigers to spend more time fighting the opposition than each other and got them to play the hustling, aggressive baseball he had learned under Hanlon. He put a stop to the harassment of Cobb by Tiger veterans that had helped hold

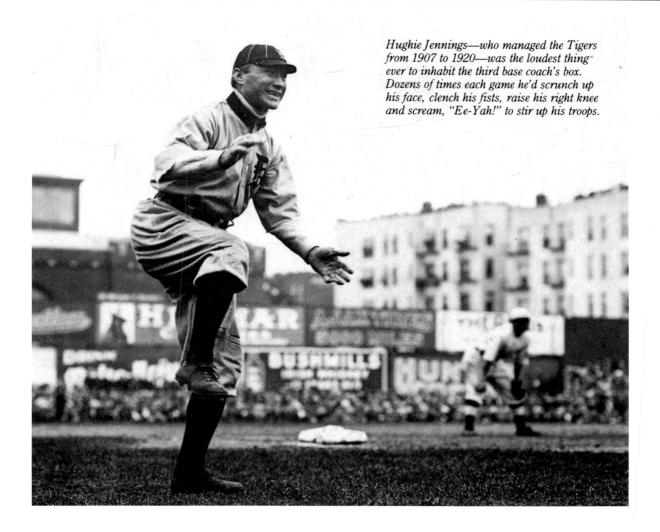

Hughie Jennings—who managed the Tigers from 1907 to 1920—was the loudest thing ever to inhabit the third base coach's box. Dozens of times each game he'd scrunch up his face, clench his fists, raise his right knee and scream, "Ee-Yah!" to stir up his troops.

the team to sixth place the year before. "He's not going to be driven off this club if I have to fire everybody else," Jennings said. "The next guy who taunts him or lays a hand on him will have to answer to me." And when one Tiger complained that Cobb was getting special treatment, Jennings replied, "You're damned right he is, and when you play like him, you'll get special treatment too." Jennings was among Cobb's favorite targets for abuse, but the diminutive Irishman held his temper in check and found a spiritual outlet for his anger. "Sometimes I think Cobb did more for my soul than anyone else," Jennings said. "I hated him so much for what he said about me that I kept going to confession to cleanse my heart."

The Tigers won pennants in 1907, 1908 and 1909, but lost each time in the World Series. AL president Ban Johnson didn't like the fact that Jennings had brought his rowdy NL style of play to the AL—and cost Johnson three Series. "We didn't seem to have much trouble in the World Series until that damn National Leaguer got into it," he said. "Then we got the hell kicked out of us." Jennings never won another pennant as a manager, though his 1915 Tigers won 100 games.

Still, he remained one of the game's most entertaining figures. He is probably best remembered for his antics in the third-base coach's box, the most famous of which was the "Ee-Yah" yell that became his nickname. It began as "That's the way," was shortened to "Way-uh" and then to "Ee-Yah." This probably wouldn't have been so distinctive, except that Jennings did it about 50 times a game, and punc-

tuated his yell by raising his arms, clenching his fists and lifting his right knee as high as he could. Jennings had become a first-class bench jockey while a player with the Orioles, once prompting Chicago Colts manager Cap Anson to ask, "Don't you ever shut up?" Jennings used his playfulness to distract the opposition, especially when the opposition was easily distracted, like pitcher Rube Waddell. According to the Tigers' Sam Crawford, Jennings would buy little toy snakes and jack-in-the-boxes, put them on the ground and yell, "Hey, Rube, look."

Cobb took the manager's job from Jennings after the 1920 season, but the 52-year-old skipper hooked on as a coach with McGraw's Giants. He was paid $25,000 a year to, as one reporter put it, "manage the man who managed the New York Giants." Jennings and McGraw led the Giants to four straight pennants and two world championships. When McGraw fell ill in 1925, Jennings essentially took over the club.

But the strain was too great, and Jennings suffered a nervous breakdown, followed by another bout of tuberculosis. He recovered and practiced law for a few years but died in 1928 from spinal meningitis.

Jennings was a winner, a man who played on five pennant winners, and coached or managed seven more. But he didn't believe in winning at any cost. He was a man whose humble beginnings shaped his managerial philosophy, one who treated his players as individuals. "It is an easy thing to bark at a man who is under you," he said. "And if you are mean enough and small enough, it may afford you some fleeting satisfaction to lord it over a fellow who because of his position cannot come back at you. But you show in this that you lack what it takes to be a leader. And in your heart of hearts you must know that the man who has given in to you is not sincere in his surrender.

"The true leader meets every man under him as an equal, then proves his right to leadership."

JENNINGS DETROIT

Although they had drastically different temperaments, Jennings and John McGraw (opposite, right) were great friends. They were roommates both during their playing days, and again when Jennings (right) was a coach for McGraw's New York Giants. Jennings' antics grabbed center stage while he was manager of the Tigers (above).

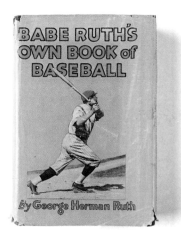

The Babe's New Game

When baseball changed, it changed quickly. In 1918 Babe Ruth of the Boston Red Sox won 13 games as a pitcher, played the outfield part-time and hit 11 home runs, enough to share the major league lead. In 1919 Ruth won nine games as a pitcher and hit 29 home runs, breaking the major league record of 24. In 1920 Ruth, playing for the Yankees, hit *54* homers. Ruth didn't choke up on the bat; he held it at the knob. He didn't punch the ball; he uppercut it. He prided himself not on line drives, but on towering fly balls of amazing length—homers measured at 500 feet or more, homers that completely cleared the Polo Grounds in New York, Comiskey Park in Chicago, League Park in Cleveland, Sportsman's Park in St. Louis.

To John McGraw, Ty Cobb and other advocates of "scientific baseball," Ruth was a heretic. The gospel of the time called for strategies designed to produce one run at a time. A *good* player, like Cobb, choked up, slashed a single, advanced on a hit-and-run or a stolen base and scored on a grounder, an outfield fly or—if his team was really lusty—on a second single. If you swung for homers, you were a selfish player, a lout. You would strike out a lot. You wouldn't get many hits, you wouldn't contribute to the team and you would defile baseball, marring the beautiful precision of offensive teamwork.

By the standards of the day, Ruth did strike out a lot: 80 times in 1920, roughly once every 7½ times at bat. So what? He batted .376, and he led

Babe Ruth shocked the baseball world with how far—and high—he could hit a baseball. Even his pop-ups were legendary. "He'd hit 'em so high that everyone on the field thought he had a chance to get it," said Casey Stengel.

Detroit's Ty Cobb showed little respect for Ruth's power game and proved that he didn't need to clear the fences to put up awesome numbers. In 1911 he hit just eight homers, but scored 147 runs and drove in 144.

the league in runs with 158 and in RBI with 137. That's *contributing*. As for marring the beauty of baseball, the fans certainly didn't think so. Attendance increased sharply in 1919, took another big jump in 1920 and followed the hitting parade as it marched triumphantly upward through the decade.

Ruth didn't exactly slow down the Yankees, who had never won a pennant before they got him from the Red Sox in one of history's greatest steals. With him, they won seven pennants and four world championships, and changed baseball forever. The strategies of scientific baseball were not lost. But it often became more sensible to play the power game—to go for big rallies with a succession of hits, climaxed, ideally, with a home run.

Although no one came close to Ruth as a home run hitter, hitting in both major leagues took off in the 1920s, and so did scoring. In 1916 the Tigers, Ty Cobb and all, led the majors in runs with 670 and in team batting at .264. In 1921 the Tigers scored 883 runs, batted .316—and finished in sixth place. The Yankees won the pennant, scoring 948 runs while batting .300 as a team—fourth highest in the American League.

With hitting like that, why bunt or play conservatively? Still, the new strategy rankled baseball's traditionalists. On May 5, 1925, Ty Cobb, who couldn't stand playing second fiddle to Ruth, told two sportswriters he would show them what a *real* hitter could do. "Gentlemen, I would like for you to pay particular attention today because for the first time in my career I will be deliberately going for home runs," said Cobb, who had never hit more than 12 homers in a season.

The Tigers were playing in St. Louis. Cobb, then 38 years old, homered to right in the first inning, hit a homer clear out of the ballpark in the second

Facing a 90-mph fastball, a batter with a swing as long as Darryl Strawberry's has to start early. Strawberry begins his move into the ball about the time it leaves the pitcher's hand, and in 1988 he was quick enough to launch a league-leading 39 home runs.

and homered again in the eighth. He also managed a double and two singles —16 total bases, still the AL record. The next day he hit two more homers. Then he proudly returned to the batting style that had made him famous, choking up on the bat and swinging for singles and doubles. For the season, Cobb totaled 12 homers. He batted .378. As far as the record shows, no one asked him why the hell he didn't keep on swinging for homers.

Ruth was a true phenom—the greatest phenom in the history of baseball, if not of all sports—but the sharp increase in home runs and extra-base hits in the 1920s can't be attributed entirely to his example. Legend has it that once owners realized that high-scoring games drew more fans, they juiced up the baseball, starting about 1920. But there was no evidence of this, and plenty of evidence to refute it; balls were tested in laboratory settings, and the new ball had no more bounce than the old.

The ball did in fact change, but for other reasons. Until 1920 the spitball and all its dirty cousins were legal. Moreover, balls were kept in play until they were lopsided—or worse. Pitchers, catchers and infielders spat tobacco juice on the ball, rubbed it in the dirt, and otherwise rendered it dark, heavy and hard to hit, particularly for distance.

Beginning in 1920, the spitter was outlawed; likewise, the licorice ball, the emery ball—the whole filthy family. Pitchers who already threw the spitter were allowed to keep throwing it, but no one else. The 17 surviving spitball pitchers—Burleigh Grimes and Stan Coveleski, to name just two—did very well. Not so most of their pitching brethren.

In 1929 *Scientific American* magazine compared the resiliency of the 1929 ball and the ball used in 1924. They came out about the same, but the

Continued on page 68

Bucky Harris

Bucky Harris managed for 29 seasons in the major leagues, more than anyone else except Connie Mack and John McGraw. Yet Harris' most memorable strategic triumph came in 1924, when, at 27, he was handling the Washington Senators in his first year as a manager.

Harris had been playing second base for the Senators since late in the 1919 season. Washington was a perennial also-ran, and word had it that Clark Griffith, the team's owner, was going to try to deal for Eddie Collins, the league's best second baseman, and appoint him manager. Harris would move to third base or perhaps to another team in a trade.

Instead, Griffith picked Harris to manage. No one was more startled than "the Boy Manager," as Harris came to be known. He quickly accepted, and to everyone's surprise, he guided the Senators to a close pennant victory over Miller Huggins' Yankees, who had won three straight pennants.

The Yankees were led by slugger Babe Ruth, who tried to intimidate the scrappy Harris during a crucial game in New York late that season. Harris scored the game's first run after sliding into second with his spikes high, and as the teams changed sides Ruth gave the young player-manager a warning. "Soon as I get on base I'll be down to second to see you," Ruth said. "You'll get on, Babe," Harris replied. "I'll see to that." He did, ordering Ruth walked with two out and no one on. As promised, Ruth tried to steal second, where Harris tagged him out and body-checked him into the infield.

The Senators faced John McGraw's New York Giants in that 1924 World Series. Walter Johnson, the great Washington pitcher, had won 23 games that season. But he was 36 years old, and the Giants beat him twice in the Series. Still, the Sen-

ators were alive going into Game 7, and Harris hoped to give Johnson one more chance.

McGraw was platooning the left-handed Bill Terry with George Kelly, who batted right, and in Game 1 Terry had already gotten a homer, a triple and a single off Johnson. In Game 7 Terry started at first base for the Giants, so Harris started right-hander Curly Ogden. After Ogden faced two batters, Harris pulled him in favor of lefty George Mogridge.

Harris hoped that McGraw would pull Terry. He did, but not until the sixth inning. The game was tied 3–3 after eight innings, and Harris brought in Johnson to pitch. "The Big Train" shut out the Giants for four innings, striking out Kelly with a runner on third in the ninth and fanning him again in the 11th with two runners on base. Washington scored in the last of the 12th to win the game and the Series.

Harris guided the Senators to their second pennant in 1925, but they lost the Series to Pittsburgh in seven games. Harris stayed with the Senators for three more seasons, then was traded to Detroit where he managed the Tigers for five years, through 1933. He handled the Red Sox in 1934, then was rehired by Griffith for another eight seasons with the Senators. He managed the Phillies for most of the 1943 season, then the Yankees in 1947 and 1948, returned to the Senators for five more seasons, and finished his long and nomadic career with the Tigers in 1956.

Hall of Fame slugger Goose Goslin called Harris "the best manager I ever played for." And Harris was Tiger Charlie Gehringer's favorite. "He was the most fair," Gehringer said. "He never second-guessed a player."

Bucky Harris, who managed to avoid the cellar despite almost three decades as a major league manager, saw his job as a fairly simple one. "There are only two things a manager needs to know: when to change pitchers and how to get along with your players," he said.

BUCKY HARRIS

Manager
Washington Senators 1924-1928,
  1935-1942, 1950-1954
Detroit Tigers 1929-1933,
  1955-1956
Boston Red Sox 1934
Philadelphia Phillies 1943
New York Yankees 1947-1948
Hall of Fame 1975

GAMES *(3rd all time)*	4,408
WINS	
Career *(3rd all time)*	2,157
Season High	97
LOSSES	
Career *(2nd all time)*	2,218
Season High	93
WINNING PERCENTAGE	
Career	.493
Season High	.636
PENNANTS	1924, 1925, 1947
WORLD CHAMPIONSHIPS	1924, 1947

In 1936, Harris didn't have a Walter Johnson to put on the mound to start the season. But it obviously didn't dampen his enthusiasm, and he led the Senators to fourth place and a 15-game improvement over 1935.

6' 2" 190 lbs.
BL TR

b 8/12/1919
d 11/12/1964

FRED HUTCHINSON
Manager

Of all the teams that have gone from chumps to champions in two seasons, none compare to the 1961 Cincinnati Reds. Driving that team of moderate talent to an exceptional performance was manager Fred Hutchinson.

Hutchinson was 95-71 as a pitcher in 11 years with the Detroit Tigers, and in 1952 he became the manager. The Tigers went from eighth place in 1952 to fifth in 1954, but Hutchinson resigned when the Tigers refused to give him a multiyear contract. In 1956 Hutchinson took the manager's post in St. Louis. The next year he was named NL Manager of the Year for leading the Cards to second place, their highest finish since 1949. When the team dropped to fifth in 1958, Hutchinson was fired.

Hutchinson began a six-year stint with Cincinnati, a second-division club in 1959 and 1960. After the 1960 season, Hutchinson and general manager Bill DeWitt cleaned house and brought some young talent to the Reds. Hutchinson knew how to soothe young players, and several of them, notably pitcher Joey Jay and third baseman Gene Freese, gave Hutchinson the best performances of their careers in 1961.

The pennant race was tight; the Reds edged the Dodgers by just four games. Hutchinson never took the tension out on his players, but that doesn't mean he didn't get frustrated. He had a history of explosive tantrums, and while plenty of managers throw chairs, Gene Mauch said of Hutchinson, "He throws whole rooms!"

Few players have ever hit the ball as hard, or as far, as the Giants' Willie McCovey. And the 6' 4" slugger didn't play favorites; in 1970 he homered in all 12 National League ballparks.

scientists found that every time a ball was hit, it lost a little bounce. That's significant, because the fatal beaning of Cleveland's Ray Chapman in 1920 had prompted a new practice of removing dirty or scuffed balls from play. Clean balls were easier for the batter to see, in addition to being bouncier. By actual count, the National League used 55,980 baseballs in 1929: nearly 100 per game. In 1930 hitting peaked—there has *never* been such a year for hitting since then—when the whole NL batted .303.

John McGraw, pining for the old days, fondly showed sportswriter Joe Vila a dirty, scuffed baseball that was the last of three—only three—used in a game in 1916. Back then, fans returned foul balls to the field, so a ball could be kept in play for a long time. McGraw liked that old ball. "The rule providing for throwing out a ball the moment it roughens or soils should be abolished," he said. "There never was a bit of sense in it. So long as the ball remains inside of the playing field and isn't ripped or torn it should be kept in use."

Hitters, however, liked the new ball, and the fans liked hitting, to the dismay of McGraw, Cobb and other purists. "The connoisseur is never in the majority," moaned *Baseball Magazine*. "The multitude appreciates the obvious and loses the finesse, even at the ballyard." In the 1920s team batting averages of .300 and above became common. In 1930 the St. Louis Cardinals had a .300 hitter at every position and three more on the bench. The 1927 Yankees—"Murderers' Row"—batted .307, scored 975 runs and boasted the AL's top three home run hitters. Ruth hit 60, Lou Gehrig hit 47 and Tony Lazzeri had 18. The Tigers, year after year, hit better than .290 as a team, yet never contended for a pennant. Logically enough, managers cut way back on bunting, stealing and the hit-and-run. Those elements of scientific baseball had been replaced by a new, simpler strategy: send 'em up and let 'em swing.

Cy Williams was among the game's first great pull hitters. He used the short right field porch in Philadelphia's Baker Bowl to win three NL home run titles during the 1920s, and was such a dead pull hitter that some managers moved their shortstops to the right of second base, thus occasioning the first "Williams Shift."

Dave Kingman struck out about once every four at-bats during his career, but when he did hit the ball, it usually went very far or very high. In a game at the Metrodome in Minneapolis, Kingman hit a ball that went up through a hole in the dome's inner lining and never came down. It was ruled a ground-rule double.

With a powerful lineup, it was hard for even the best manager to acquire much of a reputation as a clever strategist. In the eight seasons from 1936 through 1943, Joe McCarthy managed the Yankees to seven pennants and six world championships, yet he was derided by rival White Sox manager Jimmy Dykes as a "push-button manager." The Yankee buttons were Gehrig, DiMaggio, Dickey, Keller and Gordon, to name a few, and they generally did their own pushing.

As Lazzeri's homer total of 1927 indicates, home run hitting back then was not as frequent as it is today, though it was up sharply from the period preceding Ruth's entry into the big leagues. Most players had been trained to hit line drives, Ty Cobb style. Striking out was pretty shameful. Ruth led the AL in strikeouts five times, but he never fanned more than 93 times in a season. His 1,330 career strikeouts once led the majors; today he's not among the top 20. In the meantime, two generations of hitters had been born and nursed on home run hitting, and never mind the strikeouts.

The surge in slugging didn't happen overnight. As the years passed, batting averages gradually declined, while homers and strikeouts increased. In 1947 the New York Giants hit an NL record 221 homers —51 for Johnny Mize, 36 for Willard Marshall, 35 for Walker Cooper, 29 for Bobby Thomson—yet finished in fourth place. In 1956 the Cincinnati Reds tied that record as Frank Robinson hit 38 homers, Wally Post hit 36, Ted Kluszewski hit 35 and Gus Bell hit 29. The Reds contended, but finished third. In 1961 the Yankees outslugged their own dynasties of the Ruth, Gehrig and DiMaggio eras, pounding 240 homers. Roger Maris hit 61 to break Ruth's 34-year-old record, Mickey Mantle hit 54 and four

Joe DiMaggio's home run-to-strikeout ratio —361 to 369—is the best of anyone with more than 300 career homers. But in 1941 it was truly amazing—he hit 30 homers and fanned just 13 times.

other Yankees hit more than 20. That was a helluva Yankee team—another world champion. The stolen base had become a surprise play; in 1954 the Cleveland Indians and the New York Giants won pennants while stealing a mere 30 bases each.

But again, baseball was changing. Defensive play had greatly improved, partly because gloves were so much bigger and infields were smoother. New ballparks in Los Angeles, San Francisco, Houston, St. Louis and other cities had deeper fences and more foul ground, making homers harder to hit and enabling catchers and infielders to catch pop fouls that would have drifted into the stands of older, cozier parks. More and more pitchers learned to use illegal pitches: the spitter came back in force. Managers learned to use relief pitchers earlier, more often and with better effect.

No longer could teams count on a succession of hits to produce rallies. Soon teams began running again. By the 1980s, the stolen base, the bunt and the hit-and-run were even more prevalent than they had been in the Cobb era. Homers kept increasing, too—1987 stands as the record homer year for both leagues—but baseball was no longer a one-dimensional long-ball game. No one need mourn the change. Ruth's baby, the home run, still decides lots of ballgames, perhaps more than ever. And fans still love to see it. ◑

Reggie Jackson (opposite) is baseball's all-time strikeout king—with 2,697 whiffs in 21 years—but his go-for-broke swing also produced 563 career home runs and several of the game's most lucrative contracts. As Reggie said, "Taters, that's where the money is."

Miller Huggins

Miller Huggins managed the greatest player in history, Babe Ruth, and the greatest team in history, the 1927 New York Yankees. He won six pennants and three world championships, but none of them came easy.

Huggins took over the Yankees in 1918. He seemed an unlikely skipper for the big, brawling Yankee team. He stood only 5′ 4″ tall. He had a law degree from the University of Cincinnati. He was frail, moody, nervous and superstitious. Yet his baseball credentials were impeccable—13 seasons as a fine leadoff man and second baseman for the Cincinnati Reds and St. Louis Cardinals, and five seasons as the Cardinals' manager, the first four as player-manager.

But the Cards were weak, and Huggins had to use every trick he could to scrape out wins. Coaching third base one day, as most managers did back then, Huggins figured a way to get the winning run home from third base. Two were out, and a young rookie, Ed Appleton, was pitching for the rival Brooklyn Dodgers. "Hey, Bub," Huggins called to Appleton, "let me see that ball." Appleton flipped the ball to Huggins—who let it roll past as the Cardinal runner ran home.

In New York Huggins inherited a team that, like the Cardinals, had never won a pennant and didn't have the tools to contend. But owner Jake Ruppert bankrolled Huggins' efforts to improve the team. Ruppert bought Huggins the stars he needed, most of them from Harry Frazee, who stripped his superb Boston Red Sox team to finance his Broadway shows. The Yanks climbed to fourth place in 1918, Huggins' first year, and to third in 1919. Then on January 3, 1920, Ruppert bought Babe Ruth from the Bosox for $125,000. The Yankees also loaned Frazee $300,000—and took a mortgage on Fenway Park!

Ruth was only 25. He had hit a record-setting 29 homers for the Red Sox in 1919. For the Yankees, he hit 54 homers in 1920 and 59 in 1921, and lifted the Yanks to their first pennant with the help of another newly purchased Red Sox star, pitcher Waite Hoyt.

To Huggins, winning was wonderful, but managing Ruth was difficult. The Babe was a hedonist. He spent his nights drinking and whoring, and often didn't get to bed at all. Moreover, he liked company, and many of his teammates enjoyed long evenings with the playful Babe.

During spring training of 1922, a New York paper announced, "Yankees Training on Scotch." Huggins tried to rein in Ruth and his buddies, with little success. After helping the team to the 1921 AL pennant, Ruth and Bob Meusel, another star outfielder, gave Huggins a new headache. The pair defied a ban on postseason barnstorming and were suspended by Commissioner Kenesaw Mountain Landis for the first two months of the 1922 season.

Happily for Huggins, Ruppert bought two more star pitchers from the Red Sox following the 1921 season. Between them, Bullet Joe Bush and Sad Sam Jones won 39 games for the Yanks in 1922, while Hoyt won 19. Huggins brought the Yankees home in first place, one game ahead of the St. Louis Browns.

The Yanks lost the 1921 and 1922 World Series to John McGraw's Giants. McGraw was a colorful and gregarious man-about-baseball and man-about-town, and he overshadowed Huggins. In 1923 Huggins got his turn. The Yankees moved into Yankee Stadium that spring. Ruth adopted a more reasonable approach to life and rang up a memorable season—41 homers, 131 RBI, 151 runs

In his playing days, Miller Huggins was among the finest second basemen in baseball, and he led the NL four times in walks. But he wasn't cover material until he became a manager. "A manager has his cards dealt to him, and he must play them," Huggins said. In 1927 he was dealt a royal flush, and his Yankees won 110 games and finished 19 games ahead of the second-place Athletics.

scored and a .393 batting average. Yankee money delivered yet another Boston pitching ace to Huggins' rotation—Herb Pennock, who won 19 games. The "Bosox Four" of Pennock, Jones, Hoyt and Bush won 76 of the Yankees' 98 victories. The Yanks coasted home by 16 games, faced the Giants in the World Series for the third straight year and finally beat them, 4–2.

The Yanks finished second in 1924 to the upstart Washington Senators, and in 1925 Huggins' authority was sorely tested by Ruth, who was drinking, eating and carousing more than ever. On August 29, with the Yankees in seventh place, Ruth showed up a half hour late for a game. Huggins suspended him and fined him $5,000—more than most front-line players made in a season. Ruth raised hell, but Ruppert and the team's general manager, Edward G. Barrow, supported Huggins. Ruth capitulated, apologizing to his manager.

Huggins made another significant move that season. On June 2, Wally Pipp, the Yankee first baseman, was ailing, so Huggins sent young Lou Gehrig out to play first base. Gehrig played the position every day for the next 14 seasons—2,130 con-

secutive games—and rivaled Ruth as a slugger. Also moving into the lineup was center fielder Earle Combs, a great leadoff hitter.

Huggins had his team—the great Yankee "Murderers' Row." From seventh place in 1925, the Yanks edged the Cleveland Indians to win the 1926 pennant. The 1927 Yankees ran away from the league and are generally rated as the best baseball team in history. Ruth hit 60 homers that year, breaking his own record. Gehrig hit 47 and drove in 175 runs. Wilcy Moore, pioneering as a relief ace, won 19 games and saved 13 others. And the Yankees held on to edge Connie Mack's superb Philadelphia Athletics in 1928.

The Yankees were blessed with talent, and Huggins knew how to use it. He played the power game; you could almost say that Huggins and the Yankees *invented* power baseball, making the bunt and the hit-and-run back-burner strategies. Huggins handled players according to their differing personalities, goading one while giving another a pat on the back. He was a great manager of pitchers, coaxing consistently excellent seasons from his starters.

The Cardinals upset the Yankees in the 1926 World Series, but in 1927 the Yanks swept the Pirates in four and in 1928 they gave the Cardinals the same treatment. The National Leaguers were awed by the Yankee power.

The Philadelphia Athletics were not. Their lineup rivaled that of the Yankees. During the 1929 season the A's pulled ahead of the Yanks and kept on winning. Huggins tried every strategy he knew, every ploy to get more from his players. He developed a sore under his eye but refused medical treatment until he fell seriously ill in late September. He was hospitalized with severe blood poisoning and died five years later, at 50.

Gehrig said Huggins had been like a father to him. Ruth, who had contributed so much to his manager's success—and to his worries—served as a pallbearer at Huggins' funeral, at which he said, "The finest little fellow in the world has left us."

MILLER HUGGINS

Manager
St. Louis Cardinals 1913-1917
New York Yankees 1918-1929
Hall of Fame 1964

GAMES	2,570
WINS	
Career	1,413
Season High *(3rd all time)*	110
LOSSES	
Career	1,134
Season High	99
WINNING PERCENTAGE	
Career	.555
Season High *(4th all time)*	.714
PENNANTS	1921, 1922, 1923, 1926, 1927, 1928
WORLD CHAMPIONSHIPS	1923, 1927, 1928

Huggins (opposite center, with, from left, Waite Hoyt, Babe Ruth, Bob Meusel and Bob Shawkey) was once described as a "skinny scrap of a fellow who did not seem to be able to find a uniform small enough to fit him." Until he came along, the Yankees had never won a pennant; under Huggins, they won six in eight years.

Cheating

heating in baseball isn't like cheating at cards. Get caught with an ace up your sleeve and you'll be cast out of the society of friendly cardplayers. Get caught throwing a scuffball or corking a bat and you'll be welcomed as one of the boys. And you probably won't get caught, because umpires have learned to look the other way. Former ump Ron Luciano, in his book *Remembrance of Swings Past,* wrote, "In my entire minor and major league career I never caught a single pitcher doing anything illegal. I didn't want to catch a pitcher for two reasons: one, the American League didn't want me to, and two, the American League *really* didn't want me to."

In the National League, umpires Chris Pelekoudas and Shag Crawford experimented with virtue on August 18, 1968. Phil "the Vulture" Regan, the NL's top relief pitcher, was working for the Cubs, and Pelekoudas decided that three pitches Regan threw that day were illegal, and he called a ball each time. "I could feel the Vaseline on the inner lining of Regan's cap," Pelekoudas explained. Crawford said he felt the Vaseline too. The opposing pitcher, George Culver of the Reds, found a tube of Vaseline and two slippery elm tablets on the ground, and turned them in as evidence. So Warren Giles, the National League president, flew to Chicago, held a hearing and ruled in Regan's favor. "Phil has told me he did not have Vaseline or any other lubricant on his sweat band, and I believe him," Giles explained. He described Regan as a "gentleman." The umpires retreated.

Cheating has been part of baseball since professionalism crept into the game about 1870, and it is an accepted part of game strategy. The code is a strange one. Within accepted bounds, a ballplayer can cheat on the field, but that does not mean he can conduct the rest of his life dishonestly. George

Milwaukee's Lew Burdette was among baseball's most audacious spitball pitchers during the 1950s. When umpires got suspicious and asked to inspect the baseball, he'd roll it through the grass to them, thereby removing the offending moisture.

The case against Minnesota's Joe Niekro (preceding page) was ironclad. Asked to empty his pockets by umpire Dave Palermo on August 3, 1987, Niekro flipped out a five-inch emery board and a finger-shaped piece of sandpaper. There were 33,938 witnesses, and Niekro was suspended for ten days.

Bamberger, who managed the Milwaukee Brewers for five years and the New York Mets for two, explained it this way: "A guy who cheats in a friendly game of cards is a cheater. A pro who throws a spitball to support his family is a competitor."

Cheating cannot be flagrant; a pitcher can't openly scuff the ball or spit on it. In 1980 Rick Honeycutt, then with Seattle, was caught with a thumbtack sticking through a Band-Aid on his finger. "Son, take a hike," said umpire Bill Kunkel. It was a fatherly way to eject Honeycutt, and it came from an ump who had thrown a spitter or two during his own playing days. Anyway, umpire Nestor Chylak said that detecting Honeycutt's transgression "was about as difficult as spotting a whale in a bathtub." Honeycutt wasn't very smooth. As he left the mound he wiped his brow, forgetting the thumbtack, and scratched his forehead bloody.

On August 3, 1987, veteran Joe Niekro of the Minnesota Twins was caught with a five-inch emery board and a piece of sandpaper. "The guy was so blatant," said umpire Dave Palermo, "it was like a guy walking down the street carrying a bottle of booze during Prohibition." Palermo collected six balls that had been sculpted by Niekro and sent them to the league office. The opposing manager, Gene Mauch of the California Angels, viewed the exhibits with admiration. "Those balls weren't roughed up," he said. "Those balls were borderline mutilated." Niekro said he used the tools only to file his fingernails. He was suspended for ten days.

Nowadays, a manager can ask the ump to check a suspicious bat for corking. But he can only do it once a game, prompting managers to choose the right spot. Cardinal manager Whitey Herzog reasons that if he uses up his

Checking bats for cork and other illegal substances became quite common in the second half of the 1980s, and even power hitters who looked like power hitters—for example, Minnesota's 6'4", 205-pound Tom Brunansky (not shown) were suspect. Umpire Nick Bremigan checked Brunansky's bat as manager Billy Gardner and outfielder Dave Engle (above, right) looked on.

Graig Nettles is famous for an incident in which his bat broke and six super balls flew out, but he was also involved in another notorious bat-related incident. During a 1983 series between his Yankees and the Royals, Nettles noticed that George Brett had pine tar on his bat past the legal limit—18 inches from the end. Nettles told manager Billy Martin. Later that season, after Brett homered in the ninth to give the Royals a 4–3 lead over the Yanks, Martin asked that Brett's bat be checked. The bat was ruled illegal, the home run was disallowed and New York won the game.

bat check in an early inning, "everyone on the bench can go get their corked bats because the umps can't check anymore." In fact, umps have a hard time detecting a corked bat, even on close examination. Bat corkers are rarely exposed, and when they are, it is usually because of an embarrassing accident. On September 7, 1974, Graig Nettles of the Yankees homered in the first game of a doubleheader and homered again in the second inning of the nightcap. Next time up he singled, but his bat broke and six super balls bounced out. "Nettles was the first man to bounce out to the third baseman, the shortstop, and the second baseman all at once," chortled *Time* magazine. Nettles claimed he had borrowed the bat. He was called out, but it wasn't much of a penalty since the Yanks won, 1–0, on the miscreant's second-inning homer.

In 1987—a vintage year for cheating, or at least for getting caught —Billy Hatcher of the Astros broke his bat on an infield hit. The opposing third baseman, Keith Moreland of the Cubs, picked up the pieces and showed them to the umpire. The bat had been hollowed and corked. Hatcher claimed that he had borrowed the bat. He was suspended for ten days.

Baseball combines both individual and team effort, and so does cheating. On the individual side, take the confrontation between pitcher and batter. A pitcher can cheat by doctoring the ball. He can spit on it, though that is rather passé. He can put a dab of grease on it—Vaseline and K-Y Jelly have been big-league favorites. He can scuff it or scratch it, using a buckle or a hidden tool, such as sandpaper or a nail file. He has to do it subtly and artistically, so as not to embarrass the umpire. The process takes practice, and so does the pitch. Not everyone can do it. "I tried to become an im-

Although he was ejected in 1978 for throwing baseballs that had been doctored, Don Sutton got a lot of mileage from his infamous scuffball. The pitch earned him the nickname "Black & Decker" as well as a number of his 324 career wins.

Detroit slugger Norm Cash tagged 377 homers from 1958 to 1974 but took little of the credit for himself. "I owe my success to expansion pitching, a short right field fence and my hollow bats," he said.

pure pitcher but I couldn't master it," said Hank Aguirre, who got by with legal pitches during a 16-year career that ended in 1970.

Teammates help. Catchers scuff a ball by scratching it across their shin guard buckles, infielders by roughing it against the ground. When Clay Bryant coached third base for the Los Angeles Dodgers, he would occasionally sneak the infield practice ball into play, enabling the Dodger pitcher to throw two or three pitches with a worn and scuffed ball. Whitey Ford, the southpaw Yankee ace of the 1950s and 1960s, mixed turpentine, baby oil and rosin. He called it his "magic elixir," and often used a dab to get a hellacious breaking pitch. To keep the rest of the ball dry, he told Yankee infielders never to oil their gloves. Not oiling your glove is legal. Spitting on the ball is not, and at least two infielders—Nellie Fox of the White Sox and Rusty Staub of the Astros—have been caught doing it. Fox was crude; he used tobacco juice and was thrown out of the game. Staub used plain spit, and the umpires called a ball.

The scuffball is easier to throw than the spitter or its cousin, the greaseball. Veteran southpaw Mike Flanagan once gave writer Tom Boswell a demonstration. "It's the same principle as one of those flat-sided Wiffle Balls," Flanagan explained as he made successive pitches break in, out, up and down. "You hold the ball with the scuffed side opposite to the direction you want it to break. It takes no talent whatsoever. You just throw it like a mediocre fastball. The scuff gives the break."

A spitter requires more skill. The pitcher puts a dab of moisture or grease on the ball, avoiding the seams. He grips the ball with his index and middle fingers on the wet spot and his thumb on a dry spot—again, avoiding the seams. As he throws the ball he squirts it out of his fingers, preventing

Gaylord Perry played his own version of the shell game with major league umpires, challenging them to figure out in which of his many hiding spots he had stashed his illegal substance du jour. "I reckon I tried everything on the old apple but salt and pepper and chocolate sauce topping," Perry wrote in his autobiography, Me and the Spitter.

spin. As the pitch approaches the plate it drops precipitously. A knuckleball works much the same way. The knuckler is legal, but harder to master.

Just as pitchers can doctor the ball, hitters can doctor their bats. George Sisler pounded brads into his bat for harder surface. In 1922 he hit .420 for the St. Louis Browns; without the doctored bat, he might only have hit .415. Catcher Dave Rader played for the Phillies in 1979 and said a carpenter kept the team supplied with corked bats. Lots of players do it themselves, using a drill to hollow the end of the bat and filling the hole with cork, super balls or some other light material. Plastic wood, sanding and staining finish the job.

Players used to think that the resilience of the illegal filling helped the ball go farther. Scientists have tested corked bats. They agree that the ball goes farther when hit, but say it is simply because the bat is lighter, enabling the hitter to swing with more speed. That raises the question of how many homers Babe Ruth might have hit had he used the light, thin-handled bats in vogue today. Ruth used a 42-ounce bat, about ten ounces heavier than the bats favored by today's sluggers. Then again, Seattle players were admiring an old bat of Ruth's in 1983, and outfielder Dave Henderson noticed that the end was cracked, while the rest of the bat was not. "That's a plug!" said Henderson. "This bat is corked!" In deference to legend, no one opened the bat to find out.

There is risk in cheating, but to some players the benefit is well worth the risk—especially since the cost is so light. When Gaylord Perry threw his first spitball on May 31, 1964, he was a marginal relief pitcher with the San Francisco Giants, supporting a wife and two children on

$9,500 a year and fearing a demotion to the minors. "I was a power pitcher with *almost* enough power," he recalled in his autobiography. With an extra-inning game on the line, he threw his first spitball. "She dipped into the dirt like a shot quail," Perry said, and his infielders—far from disapproving— "gave me that look of pride you get from your folks on graduation day."

Casey Stengel of the Mets was the opposing manager that day. He recognized Perry's spitter and badgered the umpires to do something about it. They didn't. For 20 years, Perry kept throwing the spitter, not to mention "the mud ball, the emery ball, the K-Y ball, the Vaseline ball and the sweat ball, just to name a few." Perry won 20 games five times and won 314 games altogether—14th on the all-time list. He won two Cy Young Awards, one in each league. Opposing players and managers protested regularly, and umpires frequently inspected Perry, looking for whatever he was using on the ball that day, wherever he might be hiding it. But in all those years he was disciplined exactly once: in 1982, when he was 43 years old. He was tossed out of the game, suspended ten days and fined all of $250.

When Perry was thrown out of that game in 1982, the spitball had been illegal for 62 years. Yet his ejection was only the second in major league history. The first spitball felon was Nels Potter of the St. Louis Browns, who was tossed out on July 20, 1944, by umpire Cal Hubbard. The opposing Yankees had two men on base when Potter departed, and the Browns' relief pitcher left them there as he got out of the inning. Dizzy Dean was broadcasting the game. "Looks like ol' Hub changed pitchers just at the right time," Dean said.

Lots of pitchers, from the ordinary to the great, have won games with illegal pitches. Preacher Roe used the spitter and helped the Brook-

Continued on page 86

Atlanta Stadium

The 1965 Milwaukee Braves didn't really need any help hitting home runs. Led by Hank Aaron and Eddie Mathews, they had six players with at least 20 home runs that season, tying a major league record set by the 1961 Yankees of Roger Maris and Mickey Mantle. Then in 1966 the team moved to Atlanta and into the finest home run park in baseball. In their first season there, the Braves hit 207 homers, the fourth-highest total in NL history, and 118 of them came at home. During the five-year period from 1976 to 1980, an average of 160 home runs a season were hit in Atlanta Stadium. A distant second was Chicago's Wrigley Field with 138.

Nobody seems to know why Atlanta-Fulton County Stadium is such a haven for power hitters. It's not the stadium's dimensions, which at 330 feet down the lines, 385 in the power alleys and 402 to straightaway center are not unusual. At 1,050 feet above sea level, Atlanta is the highest city in the majors, but Dr. John Harper, professor of aerospace studies at Georgia Tech, says that isn't enough to account for the homer barrage. "I really don't have an answer, or a theory," he said.

The first home run hit in Atlanta Stadium was, naturally, hit by a guy named Aaron. Only it wasn't Hank. In an exhibition game in 1965, Hank's little brother Tommie Aaron became the first to homer in Atlanta. And when the Braves played their regular-season opener there April 12, 1966, the game was decided by a home run, as the Pirates' Willie Stargell beat the Braves with a blast in the 13th.

But it was Hank Aaron that made "the Launching Pad"—as the stadium came to be known—the site of baseball's most famous home run. By 1974 Aaron had already hit his 500th, 600th and 700th career home runs in Atlanta Stadium and was winding down his brilliant career. In his first eight seasons in Atlanta he launched 57 percent—190 of 335—of his dingers from his home pad. Entering the 1974 season, Aaron needed just one homer to tie Babe Ruth's all-time record of 714, and he got that one in his first at-bat of the season in Cincinnati. Just four days later, on April 8, the Braves played their home opener against the Dodgers, and in the fourth inning Aaron tagged Al Downing to break Ruth's record. In a 1976 nationwide poll, fans voted the homer baseball's most memorable moment.

But Aaron wasn't the only hitter who fattened his stats in Atlanta Stadium. In 1973 second baseman Davey Johnson—whose previous career high was 18 homers—hit 43, including 26 at home. Aaron smacked 40 and Darrell Evans had 41 that season, making the Braves the only team in history with three players hitting 40 or more homers in a single season. Unfortunately for Atlanta fans, all this power has translated into just two division titles and not a single pennant. The Braves were NL West champs in 1969 and 1982 but were swept in both their NLCS appearances.

Still, the home run has always been the prime cause for celebration in Atlanta Stadium, and the park's top celebrant is Chief Noc-A-Homa, who does a war dance whenever a hometown favorite hits a home run. The Chief has been moved from left field to right field and back again over the years, but when he was removed late in the 1982 season in favor of filling the 235 seats his platform occupied, the Braves went into a tailspin. He was quickly returned to the stands, and the Braves recovered to win the division by one game.

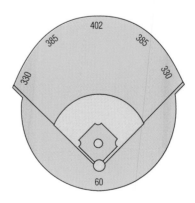

Atlanta Stadium may not be the most beautiful in baseball, but then it was built in just 50 weeks. It has also been the site of some bizarre promotions, including "Headlock and Wedlock Night," where 34 couples were married at home plate followed by an evening of pro wrestling.

Atlanta-Fulton County Stadium

521 Capitol Avenue
Atlanta, Georgia

Built 1965

Atlanta Braves, NL
  1966-present

Seating Capacity
53,043

Style
Superstructure with
natural surface

Height of Outfield Fences
10 feet

Dugouts
Home: 1st base
Visitor: 3rd base

Bullpens
Home: right field
Visitor: left field

In 1971 Kansas City's Amos Otis was nabbed when his bat broke to reveal cork and super balls, but he got off with just a warning.

On July 5, 1987, Phillies pitcher Kevin Gross complained that the balls left on the mound by Houston's Mike Scott were scuffed. On August 10 Gross was caught with a small piece of sandpaper glued to his glove and was promptly suspended for ten days.

lyn Dodgers win pennants in 1949, 1952 and 1953. Lew Burdette used it: he made little mudpies around the mound and picked up gook as he went for the rosin bag. He won 20 games twice, helped the Milwaukee Braves win pennants in 1957 and 1958, and beat the Yankees three times in the 1957 World Series. The Yankees themselves won 11 pennants and eight world championships with the help of Whitey Ford's greaseball. Don Drysdale's spitter helped the Dodgers win five pennants and three world championships. Mike Scott has never been convicted of throwing the scuffball, but he is a prime suspect. He is also one of the NL's top pitchers; he won the Cy Young Award in 1986 when he pitched the Houston Astros to a division championship and beat the Mets twice in the NL Championship Series.

Bat corkers are proud, too. Amos Otis starred for the Royals as they won AL West titles in 1976, 1977, 1978 and 1980. In 17 seasons, Otis hit 193 homers. Of his bats, Otis proudly said, "I had enough cork and super balls in there to blow away anything. Over my whole career, it probably meant about 193 home runs for me." Norm Cash, another confessed corker, hit 377 homers in 17 seasons, helping the Tigers win the world championship in 1968 and a division championship in 1972. Howard Johnson of the Mets has never been caught corking, but he became a prime suspect after hitting 36 homers in 1987; he had never before hit more than 12. "He ain't Babe Ruth," said Whitey Herzog. After opposing managers started asking umpires to check Johnson's bats, his power production declined. In 1989 Johnson again hit 36 homers, proving that either he had gone back to corking or that he never corked in the first place. Maybe Johnson will tell us after he retires, but for now the bat still looks light in his hands.

f cheating by individual players can win pennants, think what organized team cheating can do. It is legal to steal the opposing team's signals, but not with binoculars from the bleachers or from a hole in the scoreboard, as many teams have done and probably still do. At the old Polo Grounds in New York, the clubhouse was in deep center field. John McGraw, who won ten pennants as manager of the Giants from 1902 until 1932, stationed a spy with binoculars in a clubhouse window; the spy would raise or lower the shade to tell the batter whether to expect a fastball or a breaking pitch.

That sounds easy, but it's really an art. Teams change their signs, so the spy might make a catastrophic mistake. If a spy calls a curveball and the pitcher crosses him up with a fastball, the hitter—waiting for the ball to break—might fail to get out of the way of an inside hummer. Joe Medwick, a Hall of Fame slugger with the Cardinals and Dodgers of the 1930s and 1940s, was badly beaned in just such a case of mistaken spying.

Even when the spy is getting it right, he has to pick his spots. If he signals every pitch, the opposition will soon realize that their signals are being stolen and they will change them. In the heat of the AL pennant race of 1948, the Cleveland Indians went high tech, buying a rifle-range spotting scope so their man in the scoreboard could catch every sign, close up. Marshall Bossard, the groundskeeper's son, was the spy, and he knew enough to signal a pitch only once in a while. With a game on the line, Yankee pitcher Joe Page fell behind Cleveland's Joe Gordon 3 and 0 one day. The situation called for an automatic fastball, and Bossard was surprised to see the Yankee catcher call for a curve. He flashed the spy sign to Gordon, who hit the ball a mile. Before it landed in the bleachers, the whole Yankee team was pointing to the scoreboard and screaming in outrage.

Ever since he tripled his home run output to 36 in 1987, Mets third baseman Howard Johnson (above, handing his bat to St. Louis' Tony Pena) has been suspected of corking his bats. But when he hit another 36 homers in 1989, even Cardinal manager Whitey Herzog—Johnson's prime accuser—relented and suggested that Johnson's arms should be checked instead.

Don Drysdale's blond locks were the subject of numerous umpire searches throughout his Hall of Fame career, and the Dodger right-hander had only one objection. "When I have fingers run through my hair," he said, "I usually get kissed."

Preacher Roe's was another career rescued by an illegal pitch. He was 34–47 when he decided to add a new pitch in the winter of 1947, and went 93–37 after that. "If it's a good 'un," Roe said of his spitter, "it drops like a dead duck just when it crosses the plate."

The Indians won the pennant that year, and Marshall wasn't the only Bossard to contribute. Marshall and his brother Harold helped their father, Emil, tailor the field to suit the skills of the Cleveland players. "Emil was the tenth man in our lineup," said Lou Boudreau, who managed the Indians from 1942 through 1950. "I wouldn't be surprised if he helped us win as many as ten games a year."

By 1954 Al Lopez was the Indian manager. He had his job to do, and the Bossards had theirs. "We have three guys who could pull the ball down to left field—Al Rosen, Bobby Avila and Al Smith," said Harold Bossard. "That's one-third of the offense. So we decided to speed up the field down third base." They did it by hardening the dirt in front of the plate. "If the first bounce is quick and sharp the ball has a better chance of going through the infield," Emil Bossard explained. "We rolled it plenty and didn't give it much water before games, especially when we played the weaker clubs, who couldn't pull." Rosen, Avila and Smith rocketed shots past opposing third basemen all summer, and the Indians won 111 games and a pennant. Rosen, the Cleveland third baseman, played deep, knowing grounders would get to him quickly. The Pittsburgh Pirates of 1960 preferred a hard infield to help their hitters—and in Game 7 of the 1960 World Series a hard grounder caught Yankee shortstop Tony Kubek in the Adam's apple, injuring him and touching off a three-run rally that set the stage for Bill Mazeroski's dramatic, Series-winning homer in the Pittsburgh ninth.

To help bunters, good groundskeepers soften the ground in front of home plate so the ball will roll slowly. They tilt the baselines imperceptibly inward so bunts will roll fair. When the speedy Los Angeles Dodgers went to San Francisco for Game 1 of the best-of-three playoff for the 1962 National

League pennant, they found a bog around first base—the result of a Giant watering job to prevent stealing by Maury Wills, who had stolen 104 bases for the Dodgers that season. Dodger manager Walter Alston protested, and umpires ordered remedial work by the groundskeepers, but the baselines somehow stayed soft.

The Cleveland, Los Angeles and San Francisco groundskeepers were following a long tradition. Hard-throwing overhand pitchers prefer high mounds. Christy Mathewson of the New York Giants was such a pitcher, and in 1901 he was disturbed to find the mound at the Brooklyn Dodgers' Washington Park leveled—or worse. "I'm throwing from a hollow instead of off a mound," he complained to his manager, George Davis. "Never mind," replied Davis. "When we are entertaining, the box at the Polo Grounds will be built up the days you are going to pitch against Brooklyn, and you can burn them over and at their heads if you like."

If a team can tailor the home field to enhance its own strengths and sap those of opponents, why not tailor the balls, too? The Chicago White Sox of the mid-1960s had great pitching and defense but no power, so their manager, Eddie Stanky, froze baseballs overnight to deaden them. He'd take them out a few hours before the game. The covers would thaw, so the balls didn't feel cold, but the cork and rubber inside would remain cold and inelastic. "You had to wipe the mildew off the balls before the game," recalled catcher Jerry McNertney. Minnesota, with Harmon Killebrew, Tony Oliva and Bob Allison in the lineup, was one of the teams that got the frozen-ball treatment in Chicago. "When our power hitters made contact, it was like hitting a rock and the ball didn't go anywhere," said Twins pitcher Jim Kaat.

Dodger reliever Jay Howell claimed that he used pine tar merely to improve his grip during a rainy Game 3 of the 1988 NLCS against the Mets, but he was suspended for three games anyway under baseball's rule 8.02(b) prohibiting the use of foreign substances. Howell's suspension was later cut to two days.

Improving the Odds

Players deny it, umpires ignore it, the leagues embark on periodic crusades against it, but cheating is as traditional as hot dogs. Balls are greased, spit on, tarred, scuffed, cut and maimed in ways that stagger the imagination. Bats are drilled and plugged for greater power. It's all testimony to one of baseball's most sacred ethics: it ain't cheating if you don't get caught.

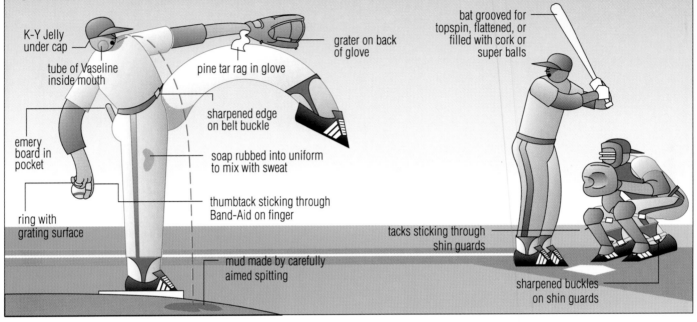

K-Y Jelly under cap

tube of Vaseline inside mouth

pine tar rag in glove

grater on back of glove

bat grooved for topspin, flattened, or filled with cork or super balls

sharpened edge on belt buckle

soap rubbed into uniform to mix with sweat

emery board in pocket

thumbtack sticking through Band-Aid on finger

ring with grating surface

mud made by carefully aimed spitting

tacks sticking through shin guards

sharpened buckles on shin guards

heating goes way back. In the 1880s the flamboyant Mike "King" Kelly of the Chicago White Sox took shortcuts in running the bases when the lone umpire was looking elsewhere. Spiking became so savage that spiked shoes were banned for several years. The Baltimore Orioles of the 1890s were downright dirty. They spiked opposing players with relish. And when a runner tagged up at third to score after a fly ball was caught, John McGraw, Baltimore's third baseman, would subtly grab the runner's belt for a second or two, holding him up long enough so the outfielder could throw him out at the plate. One of McGraw's victims was Pete Browning of Louisville, who got back by unfastening his belt buckle and scoring while McGraw held the belt. After the Orioles played two games in New Orleans against the local minor league team, McGraw was described in a New Orleans newspaper as "a rough, unruly man, who is constantly playing dirty ball. He has the vilest tongue of any ball-player. On the local grounds he has demonstrated his low training, and his own manager knows that, while he is a fine ball-player, yet he adopts every low and contemptible method that his erratic brain can conceive to win a play by a dirty trick."

On the Orioles, McGraw's tactics were the norm. The Baltimore groundskeeper, Tom Murphy, let the outfield grass grow tall so that Oriole outfielders could stash extra balls out there. When a ball was hit in the gap, the Oriole fielder would ignore it, pick up a stashed ball and hold the hitter to a single.

McGraw and Ty Cobb, another player who knew how and when to take a shortcut on the bases and use his spikes to advantage, had reputations as baseball devils. Connie Mack, on the other hand, was regarded as a saint, particularly during his half-century as manager and owner of the

Catchers like Elston Howard could be valuable allies in a pitcher's attempts to cheat. Howard helped Whitey Ford—who once wrote an article entitled "Confessions of a Gunkball Artist"—by loading the ball up with mud or rubbing it against the sharpened buckle of his shin guard.

Current baseball rules forbid pitchers from putting their hands to their mouths while they are standing on the mound, but once in a while it's so cold that umpires rescind the ban to help pitchers keep their hands warm. The Dodgers' Fernando Valenzuela took advantage of one such opportunity.

Philadelphia Athletics. As a catcher in the 1880s and 1890s, Mack was one of the first receivers to move in close behind the batter. He invented a new trick—tipping the hitter's bat to ruin his swing. "I was kinda tricky," Mack recalled decades later. "We got away with a lot back in the days when we played with only one umpire." Mack's first managing job was with the Pittsburgh Pirates in 1894, and it was he, not Eddie Stanky, who first used frozen baseballs. Years later, George Moreland, a Pittsburgh baseball statistician, described Mack's technique to author Frederick G. Lieb: "Connie contrived to work the frozen balls into the game while the visiting team was at bat, and then substituted the unfrozen variety when the Pittsburgh club had its innings at the plate."

Rogers Hornsby was the NL's premier hitter of the 1920s; many consider him to be the greatest NL hitter of all time. Hornsby was known as much for his blunt way of speaking as for his hitting, and in his autobiography he included a chapter entitled "You've Got to 'Cheat' to Win." "I've 'cheated' or watched someone on my team 'cheat' in practically every game," Hornsby wrote. "When I played second base I used to trip, kick, elbow or spike anybody I could. If a big-league ballplayer doesn't like cutting the corners or playing with 'cheaters,' then he's as much out of place as a missionary in Russia."

Even fans sometimes get into the act. Fans of McGraw's old Orioles —and Cub fans, several generations later—brought small mirrors to the ballpark and used them to flash sun into the eyes of opposing fielders just as they prepared to catch the ball. In the old days, overflow crowds were allowed to stand in the outfield, behind ropes. In September 1922 the Yankees came to St. Louis for a crucial series against the Browns, who for once were contend-

Houston's Mike Scott called it a split-finger fastball, but a lot of hitters—most of whom couldn't touch it—called it a scuffball. In 1986 Scott fanned 306 batters—more than twice his previous career high—but survived dozens of investigations into his pitching techniques.

ing for the pennant. As Whitey Witt, the Yankee left fielder, camped under a fly ball, a hard-throwing fan conked Witt with a pop bottle, knocking him cold. The Yanks protested, but the official ruling was that Witt stepped on a bottle and it flipped up and hit him.

Not all major leaguers lack virtue. Pitcher Al Worthington quit the White Sox in 1960 when he discovered that his team was stealing signs through the scoreboard. "Baseball is a wonderful game," Worthington said. "When it's not played on the up and up, it's time to quit." Worthington returned to the majors in 1963, and led the AL in saves in 1968. Among players who remember him, Worthington is considered a curiosity. More typical was the advice given by George Bamberger, the Orioles' pitching coach in the 1970s, to pitcher Ross Grimsley. "If you can cheat," Bamberger said, "I wouldn't wait one pitch longer." ◗

Caught on a technicality, Kansas City's George Brett (opposite) threw one of the game's most famous tantrums in 1983 after a home run he hit was negated because he had applied pine tar too far up the handle of his bat. "He was a madman," said umpire Joe Brinkman (holding Brett back). "I can still see his bulging eyes and red face. It didn't seem right to take away his homer because of a little pine tar. But rules are rules."

Smart Moves

No team can win without good management, and for seven years the Brooklyn Dodgers had two of the best executives in baseball history: Branch Rickey and Walter O'Malley. They worked side by side, and they couldn't stand each other. Rickey finally left, selling his Dodger stock to O'Malley in a deal that seemed entirely in Rickey's favor. As things turned out, it was O'Malley who prospered from the transaction, and O'Malley who succeeded Rickey as baseball's most progressive, imaginative and controversial baseball owner.

O'Malley ran the Dodgers from 1950 until 1970, when he stepped down as president in favor of his son, Peter. Altogether, Rickey, O'Malley or both ruled the Dodgers for 26 years, a period in which they won ten pennants and four world championships. They tied for the National League pennant two other seasons—1946 and 1951—and lost playoffs to the St. Louis Cardinals and New York Giants, respectively.

The Rickey-O'Malley era began in 1943 when Rickey joined the Dodgers as general manager; the wealthy but obscure O'Malley was already in place as the team's general counsel. A year later they became partners, each buying 25 percent of the Dodgers; industrialist John J. Smith bought another 25 percent and acted as silent partner, leaving Rickey and O'Malley in charge. The partnership ended in 1950. By then Rickey was 68, and he saw an opportunity to get top dollar for his shares from O'Malley, who at 47 was itching to run the Dodgers—and to get rid of Rickey. Smith had died, and

Brooklyn Dodger owner Walter O'Malley (opposite) once said that the team's fans "are more important than the stockholders, the officials, the players, or anybody else." Nonetheless, in 1958 he moved the club to Los Angeles.

Some of the game's greatest—and most volatile—figures ran the Dodgers in the 1940s. Walter O'Malley (right) was positioning himself to gain majority control of the franchise, general manager Branch Rickey (left) was stockpiling the Dodger farm system with talent and field manager Leo Durocher (center) was trying desperately to give Brooklyn its first world championship.

O'Malley, who had made a considerable fortune in other enterprises, sold those holdings and used the proceeds to buy both Rickey's and Smith's shares. Rickey took $1,050,000 of O'Malley's money and moved to Pittsburgh to become general manager of the Pirates.

Rickey and O'Malley changed the face of baseball. Rickey already had changed a lot of it during his 25 years with the St. Louis Cardinals, where he founded the farm system and showed how a team in a small market could win and prosper. With the Dodgers, Rickey built the first modern spring training complex, a multidiamond facility at Vero Beach, Florida, that other teams are still copying four decades later. More important, he integrated baseball, bringing Jackie Robinson aboard in 1947 and following in 1948 with catcher Roy Campanella and in 1949 with pitching ace Don Newcombe. Characteristically, Rickey's historic step didn't just help blacks or society or baseball's reputation. It also helped the Dodgers win more pennants and make more money, because all three players turned out to be stars.

Mostly because he broke the color line, Rickey is regarded as a saint. O'Malley is regarded as a devil because he moved the Dodgers to the West Coast in 1958 and persuaded the Giants to come along and settle in San Francisco. To Dodger and Giant fans, and thousands of other baseball traditionalists, the moves were treasonous, inexcusable. Many fans have never forgiven O'Malley, who died in 1979 with the reputation of a cold-blooded Scrooge. In fact, he was more amiable than Rickey and certainly no thriftier; generations of ballplayers could attest to Rickey's miserly ways. But baseball resents change, and the changes wrought by O'Malley hurt too much, particularly in New York.

Wally Moon made an immediate impact after being traded to the L.A. Dodgers by St. Louis in 1959. His homers over the 42-foot fence just 250 feet away in left field became known as "Moon Shots," and L.A. went from seventh place to a world championship.

In fact, O'Malley carried baseball forward. If Rickey and Robinson pushed baseball into the 20th century, O'Malley propelled it toward the 21st: he encouraged television coverage of baseball. Rickey and others opposed it, accurately predicting that fans in smaller cities would stop supporting local minor league teams if given an opportunity to watch big-league games on TV. The minors shrank drastically but they did not die, and today virtually no one would argue for TV blackouts in minor league cities.

O'Malley also opened the West to major league baseball, a move that was ludicrously overdue. He built a large, comfortable ballpark, accessible by freeway and with plenty of parking, thus inviting suburban fans, and he equipped it with lots of rest rooms and other amenities so families would feel safe and welcome, as well as entertained. Traditionalists say that baseball was better off when all the ballparks were small, intimate and urban. Fans disagree; as team after team has copied Dodger Stadium, more or less, with modern facilities of their own, attendance has soared.

Baseball has prospered, and the Dodgers have prospered most of all. Year after year they have led the majors in attendance. Since moving into Dodger Stadium in 1962, they have averaged nearly 2.6 million a year in home attendance. In 1978 they became the first team to draw 3 million at home. They did it six times during the 1980s, more than all the other big-league teams put together.

To critics, all this success smacks of greed. Sportswriters like to dream of teams that win without undue concentration on the bottom line. They point to the Kansas City Royals, who have posted a consistently superb record in baseball's smallest market and, in 1990, somehow came up with $13 million

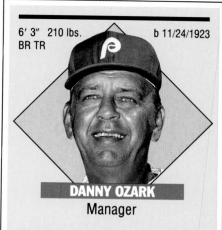

6' 3" 210 lbs.   b 11/24/1923
BR TR

DANNY OZARK
Manager

After he survived Omaha Beach and the Battle of the Bulge, there wasn't much in the NL East that could rattle Danny Ozark. Not even an overpaid, undisciplined band of Phillies.

The Phillies that Ozark led to NL East titles in 1976, 1977 and 1978 were hardly America's team. The roster included flakes like Tug McGraw and Jay Johnstone, a silent pitching marvel named Steve Carlton, and blue-collar superstars like Mike Schmidt and Bob Boone.

Ozark had spent 31 years in the Dodger organization, making the majors only as a coach. Moving to the Phillies as manager in 1973, he played his hand lightly, adjusting his style to fit that of each player. He just wasn't the drill-sergeant type.

"Don't get me wrong, I like to win," he said. "It's just that it can be done with more grace and fun. And to have fun, you have to have a close association with your players. Any manager who says he treats all his players alike is full of shit. My rules stretch like a rubber band for each one."

It may not have worked with many teams, but it did with the Phils. The players appreciated the freedom. "If Danny has any weaknesses," said slugger Greg Luzinski, "it's that he gives major-league players more credit than they deserve." But after the Phillies lost three straight NLCS and then dropped to fifth in 1979, the man they called "Ozark Ike" got the axe. He resurfaced in 1984 as manager of the Giants but lasted just 56 games.

After O'Malley announced the Dodgers would be moving to L.A., most fans stayed away from Ebbets Field, while others contemplated more drastic action. According to author Peter Golenbock, a fan named Willie Crane wanted to kill O'Malley. "He figured if he shot him, the Dodgers wouldn't move," said a fellow Dodger fan.

to sign free-agent relief ace Mark Davis to a four-year contract. The Royals' owner, Ewing Kauffman, a civic-minded millionaire—maybe billionaire—has always been willing to operate his team in the red. Gene Autry has spent freely on his beloved California Angels, and Tom Yawkey used to operate the Boston Red Sox in the same open-handed spirit. But baseball can't depend on largess. Free agency has pushed costs into the stratosphere, and most teams have to make money in order to compete. Without a decent balance sheet, a team can't afford top-rank players and can't finance a good player development system—the scouts and minor league farm clubs that find, train and bring along stars of the future. Without all this—without good players—no team can succeed for long, no matter how skillful its manager, no matter how innovative his strategies.

The Dodgers have everything going for them. They operate in the nation's second-largest market. Their ballpark is ideally located. They have a large and loyal following. As things stand, their management will have to row backwards for the team to slip. These advantages did not fall in the team's lap. They accrued from the courage and foresight of Walter O'Malley.

Legend has it that the Dodgers were making lots of money in Brooklyn and had no reason to desert Ebbets Field. O'Malley, so goes the legend, gave Brooklyn and New York an ultimatum: build me a new stadium at city expense or I'll leave. Los Angeles, say these critics, gave Dodger Stadium to O'Malley in order to lure him. None of these claims is true.

Ebbets Field held 32,000. It had become run-down and could not be expanded. The neighborhood, a source of pride when the park was built in 1913, had deteriorated. Parking was hopelessly inadequate. Families were

reluctant to attend games, particularly at night—and baseball was being played more and more at night. The Dodgers won the pennant in 1949 and drew 1,633,747 fans. They won again in 1956, yet drew only 1,213,562.

O'Malley could have waited for the team to decline before acting, but he did not. "Look at it this way," he said. "Brooklyn draws a million people. Milwaukee [then in the NL] draws two and a quarter million. Results: One, they can pay their players more. Two, they can absorb more farm club losses. Three, they can have more front-office talent. Four, they can buy more bonus players. The momentum is Milwaukee's. Obviously, we have deteriorated into a noncontending ballclub. I decided that the thing to do was get my new stadium and get in a competitive position—get the customers who could give me the money to compete again."

O'Malley admired the geodesic dome, invented by Buckminster Fuller, and suggested that the Dodgers build a stadium with a transparent dome. He was a decade ahead of his time—baseball's first domed stadium, in Houston, opened in 1965—and he was ridiculed for the idea. "Oh, give me a home, with a plexiglass dome," sang sportswriters at the annual dinner of the New York chapter of the Baseball Writers Association of America.

O'Malley wanted a stadium built, owned and paid for by the Dodgers. He first chose a site around the Long Island Rail Road station in Brooklyn. Plots of land within the site—much of it slum—were owned by a number of businesses and individuals. If every owner had negotiated individually with O'Malley, prices would have soared out of reach. So he asked the city to condemn the land for redevelopment, using the urban renewal laws. O'Malley then would have bought the land at a reasonable price and built his stadium. The New York City fathers refused, ruling that a baseball stadium did not fit

Continued on page 102

O'Malley's dream stadium became a reality in 1962 as Dodger Stadium opened as the only privately financed major league park since Yankee Stadium in 1923. But it wasn't easy. Eight million cubic yards of earth had to be moved before construction began on what became known as "Taj O'Malley."

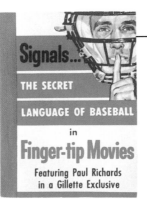

Signals...

THE SECRET

LANGUAGE OF BASEBALL

in

Finger-tip Movies

Featuring Paul Richards
in a Gillette Exclusive

Paul Richards

Manager Paul Richards never seemed to be around to ride the tide of success when the teams he built came of age, but he was the man who made the tide rise in the first place. A good-field, no-hit catcher who had played 4F ball with the Detroit Tigers during the war, Richards managed the Chicago White Sox from 1951 to 1954, always finishing in the first division. In 1955 he became both manager and general manager for the Baltimore Orioles—the St. Louis Browns masquerading as a real baseball team—and turned them into contenders by the time he left in 1961. Richards built the Orioles' farm system from scratch and filled the pipeline with the talent that would make Baltimore a dynasty for years to come.

Perhaps Richards' most important legacy was his masterful handling of pitchers. Knuckleballer Hoyt Wilhelm seemed washed up when he met Richards at Baltimore in 1958. In the following ten seasons, Wilhelm posted an ERA under 2.00 six times. Hal Newhouser was 34–52 lifetime when he met Richards in 1943. Over the next five seasons, he won 118 games. The Richards magic also saved the careers of Dutch Leonard, Billy Loes, Saul Rogovin and Virgil Trucks, who said, "Everything I know came from Paul."

Richards worked tirelessly with his players. No tiny hitch in a batter's swing or flaw in a fielder's footwork escaped his attention. A perfect example is the way he taught young second baseman Marv Breeding how to turn the double play. "He must have shown Marv how to do it 500 times," said coach Lum Harris. "Then one day Breeding got it, just like that. The 501st time."

"Everybody today knows about the same amount of baseball," said Richards. "Some managers just have a little more patience and ambition to expose their ballplayers to it."

Richards had no patience with laziness or mental errors, though, and once refused to let his team shower after a poor game. Another time, in between games of a doubleheader, he hit ground balls to a shortstop who had made three errors in the opener. His players didn't always like him, but he always got their respect—and their best performance. Once he dressed down an outfielder who wasn't hitting. The player then came up with a hot bat but complained about his manager to the press. Said Richards: "If he gets sore enough at me to hit .300, that's just fine."

An inside-baseball manager in a slugging era, Richards was an anachronism. He presaged current strategy by regularly bringing in left-handed pitchers to face left-handed batters. He sometimes intentionally walked a pitcher with two outs so that the leadoff batter could not lead off the next inning. And if he did get on, he would not be able to steal because the pitcher was clogging up the bases ahead of him. Sometimes accused of playing the percentages like a machine, Richards was in fact an innovator. In a 1951 game at Fenway Park, he moved his pitcher to third base, brought in a left-hander to get Ted Williams out and then moved the first pitcher back to the mound. His most famous innovation was the gargantuan mitt his Oriole catchers used to handle Hoyt Wilhelm's knuckleball. "I may win by the book," preached Richards, "but I'll be damned if I'm going to lose by it." He never put a pennant under his belt, but Paul Richards was no loser.

PAUL
RICHARDS

Manager
Chicago White Sox 1951-1954,
   1976
Baltimore Orioles 1955-1961

GAMES	**1,836**
WINS	
Career	**923**
Season High	**91**
LOSSES	
Career	**901**
Season High	**97**
WINNING PERCENTAGE	
Career	**.506**
Season High	**.628**

Even a fine judge of baseball talent like Paul Richards (above, right) sometimes misses. The White Sox spent over $100,000 to sign pitchers Gus Keriazakos (left) and Gar Hamlen (center), yet neither won a game for Chicago. As a catcher (below), Richards had one of the best arms—and the oddest squat—in the majors.

Heading West

In the off season of 1957-58, two of the most hallowed baseball dynasties pulled up stakes to seek greener financial pastures on the Pacific Coast. New Yorkers were outraged at losing both of their NL franchises, the Giants and the Dodgers, but no one could argue the economics. Stadium capacities and attendance figures from five seasons before and after the moves leave no doubt.

the urban renewal definition of a "public purpose" facility. Since then, city after city has used taxpayers' money to build ballparks; New York eventually built Shea Stadium for the Mets and renovated Yankee Stadium. That is much more than O'Malley asked, but he was turned down—more, he was vilified.

About that time, Los Angeles began seriously shopping for a big-league baseball franchise. It was about time; the major leagues had moved as far west as Kansas City, but no farther, and baseball's southern boundary ran from St. Louis to Washington, D.C. The L.A. city fathers hoped to get a raggedy team like, maybe, the Washington Senators. They were astounded, and delighted, when the illustrious Dodgers expressed interest.

In L.A., O'Malley quickly found the perfect stadium site: Chavez Ravine, a huge and largely deserted expanse surrounded by freeways. Los Angeles did what New York would not, condemning the land so the Dodgers could buy it, though approval eventually had to come through a public referendum, and O'Malley had to pay exorbitantly for the last few lots on his site. The Dodgers—not the city, but the Dodgers—built Dodger Stadium. For all the talk of O'Malley's extortionate ways, it was the first privately financed big-league park built since Yankee Stadium in 1922.

To be sure, O'Malley was a consummate businessman. He tried to work the political angles in New York, and when that failed, he worked the political angles in Los Angeles. Realizing that he needed a nearby rival to attract fan interest, and another West Coast team to defray travel expenses for other NL teams, he arranged a marriage between Horace Stoneham, the genial owner of the New York Giants, and the eager city of San Francisco.

The Dodgers and Giants moved west in 1958. New York was horrified. No one much blamed Horace Stoneham, a beloved baseball man who had inherited the Giants from his father. No one forgave Walter O'Malley, a paunchy businessman who had made his original fortune outside baseball. "For such villainy there had to be a villain," wrote *Sports Illustrated.* "O'Malley was from central casting."

In Los Angeles, hearts were kinder. While awaiting their new stadium, the Dodgers played in the Los Angeles Coliseum. It was built for every sport except baseball, and it was a dreadful facility with a left field fence only 251 feet from home plate. From O'Malley's standpoint, it had one redeeming feature: it seated 90,000 people. But those 90,000 seats were backless benches, none of which were in the shade. In 1958, the first year of the Los Angeles Dodgers, the team finished seventh. Nevertheless, 1,845,556 fans poured into the Coliseum to watch them.

So much for the notion that West Coast fans weren't really "big league." Anyway, O'Malley made sure that the Dodgers' eventual home would be more accommodating—more so, in fact, than many baseball men thought necessary, even though professional football was making inroads on the national pastime. "Why should we treat baseball fans like cattle?" O'Malley asked. "I came to the conclusion years ago that we in baseball were losing our audience and weren't doing a damn thing about it. Why should you leave your nice, comfortable, air-conditioned home to go out and sweat in a drafty, dirty, dingy baseball park? Why, when I came to the Dodgers, I spent a quarter of a million dollars just to change the urinals, and Branch Rickey, who was the general manager, nearly had a stroke. He couldn't comprehend spending that much money on the customers when we could spend it on ballplayers."

Once Jackie Robinson (left) broke baseball's color line and became Rookie of the Year in 1947, a steady stream of black players was brought up to the major league Dodgers by Branch Rickey and Walter O'Malley. In 1948 catcher Roy Campanella (right) hit the majors, and in 1949 pitcher Don Newcombe arrived, winning 17 games and giving the Dodgers another Rookie of the Year. In all, the trio won five MVP awards.

By the spring of 1957, O'Malley (center, with manager Walter Alston, right) was talking to the press about a possible franchise shift to the West Coast. He strengthened his hand by trading the Dodgers' Fort Worth, Texas, farm club to Philip Wrigley for the Cubs' farm club in—you guessed it—Los Angeles. With it, Rickey got a ballpark, although his Dodgers never played in it.

Walter O'Malley died in 1979, but the Dodger machine he built kept right on rolling—and stayed in the family. Minutes after pitcher Steve Howe (opposite) and catcher Steve Yeager celebrated the Dodgers' World Series win over the Yankees in 1981, Walter's son Peter accepted the world championship trophy from Commissioner Bowie Kuhn.

O'Malley wound up spending money on both. His stewardship went far beyond the move to L.A. Much as he loathed Rickey—he would not permit Rickey's name to be spoken in the Dodger office—O'Malley built on the innovations that Rickey had brought to the Dodgers. He expanded and improved the spring training site at Vero Beach. Lacking Rickey's baseball background, he put the baseball part of the operation in capable, experienced hands, notably those of veteran business manager Buzzy Bavasi and scout extraordinaire Fresco Thompson.

The Dodgers kept on winning and kept on drawing fans. O'Malley ran a tight ship, worked hard and showed a human side that got little public attention. When Bobby Thomson of the Giants hit the historic home run that beat the Dodgers in the 1951 pennant playoff, O'Malley tried to comfort the distraught Dodger pitcher, Ralph Branca. When an auto accident paralyzed Roy Campanella in 1958, O'Malley paid his medical bills and hired him as a community relations specialist.

Nevertheless, O'Malley continued to be seen as a heartless beast consumed by greed. He was typecast, and he knew it. Still serving as chairman of the Dodgers, he died on August 9, 1979, at the age of 75. Almost to the end, some of his fellow owners whispered that he ran major league baseball behind the scenes. But they paid him the ultimate compliment. They copied the way he ran a baseball team. ◗▮

Spring Training

ince 1870, when the Chicago White Stockings and Cincinnati Red Stockings opened camps in New Orleans, baseball teams have headed for warmer climates to prepare for the coming season. It's a special time, when all teams are contenders, all rookies are potential starters, and hope does indeed spring eternal.

It's also a time when the game truly gets back to basics, where players ease into the rhythm of the long season by revisiting baseball's fundamentals. Over and over they slide, bunt, throw and hit, in ballparks so small they often take time during games to chat with fans. Pitchers build up their legs with windsprints under the hot sun in Florida and Arizona, and hitters rediscover their timing with thousands of swings in the batting cage.

It's baseball in its most relaxed form for one simple reason—the games don't count.

Bo Jackson (below) and his Kansas City Royals' teammates train in their state-of-the-art facility at Boardwalk and Baseball, a 135-acre tract in Baseball City, Florida. The camp—where the Royals minor league teams also train—includes six full-sized fields, while the adjacent amusement park offers thrill rides and live entertainment. In 1959, the Phillies could fill up on fish for a buck.

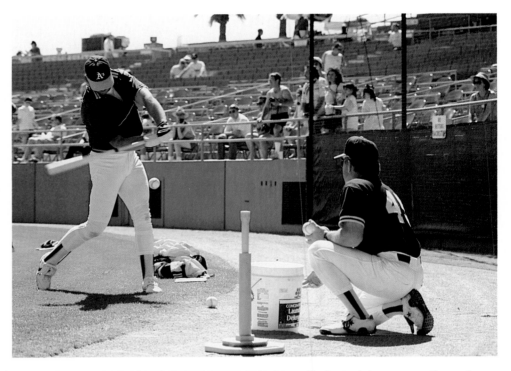

Spring training means a flurry of activity on several fields at once, and coaches with clipboards (top, left) decide who does what and where. It also means regaining your timing and your stroke, as Oakland shortstop Walt Weiss (above) gets a hand from coach Mike Paul. For catchers like Atlanta's Matt Stark (left) it's relearning the fine art of scooping up bunts. In Plant City, Florida (below), the Reds keep things close at hand with four diamonds within shouting distance of each other.

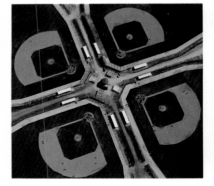

It's a spectator sport from both sides of the fence for the Red Sox in Winter Haven (above) and for Braves fans in West Palm Beach (below).

Execute 100 rundowns (Seattle Mariners, left) in March and you may get it right in October. A walk through the palms ended the Dodgers' day in Vero Beach in 1965 (below).

Masters of the Mound

Appropriately, reliever Joe Page was in the middle of the celebration when the Yankees won the 1947 World Series over the Dodgers. Page had won 14 games and saved 17 more during the regular season, then rescued the Yanks in Game 7 of the Series with five innings of shutout relief. "When he came in," said teammate Eddie Lopat, "the other team was dead."

The Yankees' Goose Gossage (preceding page)—whose fastball was once clocked at 99.4 mph—epitomized the flame-throwing relief ace of the 1970s. In 1976 the White Sox tried to make him a starter, and he went 9–17 with a 3.94 ERA. The next season, used exclusively in relief by the Pirates, he went 11–9 with 26 saves and a 1.62 ERA.

P itching—the strategy of pitching—has changed more in the past 20 years than any other element of the game. It has had to change, and it will continue to, because umpires and rule-makers tend to act in the hitter's favor whenever pitching gains the edge. The 1968 season was "the year of the pitcher"—a throwback to the dead-ball era. Composite earned run averages were 2.98 in the American League, 2.99 in the National League; by comparison, in 1987 only four pitchers in both leagues had ERAs under 3.00. After pitchers put the fans to sleep by dominating the game in 1968, rulemakers reduced the height of the mound from 15 inches to 10 and tightened the strike zone. The lower mound took the edge off power pitching by overhand fastballers like Bob Gibson and Denny McLain. Officially, the strike zone now extends from the uniform letters to the top of the knees. Actually, it's smaller than that. Umpires call anything much above the belt a ball because, they say privately, otherwise hitters wouldn't hit much.

By far the biggest change has been the increased use of relief pitchers. Today it is not unusual for a team to use four or five pitchers, even in a low-scoring game. Not too many years ago, starters were *never* yanked until they were hit hard. To be sure, a pitcher might be pulled for a pinch hitter. But relieved because he had pitched five or six or seven good innings or had thrown 100 pitches or looked tired or because a relief specialist was rested and ready? Never!

It is hard to understand why for so many years managers were reluctant to use relievers. Tradition had a lot to do with it. Starting pitchers were, by definition, the team's best pitchers. A starter was measured not only by his speed or his repertoire, but also by his stamina. He was *supposed* to finish.

Relief pitching has become so ingrained in baseball that now pitchers—like Baltimore's Gregg Olson—come out of college as relief specialists. But none has ever come out quite the way Olson did: he rode a blistering fastball and a knee-buckling curve to an AL rookie record 27 saves and a 1.69 ERA in 1989.

On May 1, 1920, at Braves Field in Boston, Joe Oeschger of the Braves and Leon Cadore of the Brooklyn Dodgers dueled to a 1–1 tie, called on account of darkness—after 26 innings. If that happened today, the pitchers might be hospitalized in the orthopedic ward, and their managers in the psychiatric ward. But neither pitcher was crippled by the experience. Both won 15 games that season; the next year, Oeschger won 20, and Cadore won 13.

That's an extreme example. Let's fast-forward 30 years or so. Casey Stengel's Yankees wouldn't have won in 1949 without reliever Joe Page, who had 13 wins and 27 saves. There was no Cy Young Award back then, but Page finished third in the Most Valuable Player voting, tops among pitchers. In 1950 relief ace Jim Konstanty of the Phillies was named MVP of the National League; he was 16–7 with 22 saves, and the Phils won the pennant. In 1959 reliever Elroy Face of the Pirates went 18–1 with 10 saves and was recognized as a bullpen marvel. Knuckleballer Hoyt Wilhelm earned renown pitching in relief for nine teams from 1952 through 1972; he was elected to the Hall of Fame in 1985.

Nevertheless, starters were still the top dogs. A few relievers stood out in 1968, notably Phil "the Vulture" Regan of the Cubs, a spitballer who rang up 10 wins and 25 saves. By and large, however, the managers of 1968 let their starters finish. Juan Marichal of the Giants went 26–9 with a 2.43 ERA and pitched 30 complete games; Bob Gibson of the Cardinals went 22–9, 1.12, and Denny McLain of the Tigers went 31–6, 1.96, and both pitched 28 complete games. The whole Tiger staff totaled only 29 saves, yet Detroit ran away with the pennant.

Now, jump to 1989. Toronto won the AL East with only 12 complete games for the whole staff. Ditto San Francisco, champion of the NL West.

Washington's Firpo Marberry had a great fastball, but not much else, so Clark Griffith turned him into baseball's first great relief pitcher. Marberry set a major league record of 15 saves, leading the Senators to the AL pennant in 1924, and he saved two more as Washington beat the Giants in the World Series.

Hoyt Wilhelm didn't make it to the majors until he was 29, but when he finally got there, he stayed for 21 years and a record 1,070 games—all but 52 in relief. Wilhelm was unique, however, as he depended on the knuckleball—baseball's hardest pitch to catch—and a pitch that doesn't lend itself to relief situations, where a passed ball can mean an instant loss.

Pittsburgh's Roy Face (right, with Tom Seaver looking on) is famous for his 18–1 season in 1959. But the 5' 8" forkball artist was at his best in the 1960 World Series and earned three saves for the Pirates in their upset win over the Yankees.

Only 483 complete games were pitched in the major leagues, a record low. Saves totaled 1,069, a record high. Ten of the 26 big-league teams boasted a closer who compiled at least 30 saves. Until 1965 no pitcher in the history of baseball had 30 saves in a season; until 1934, no team did. Those numbers come from recalculating old records; the save didn't even become an official statistic until 1969.

Talk about a strategic change! Going way back, the Boston Red Sox won the pennant in 1904 with only one save for the whole staff; Cy Young earned it, on top of his 26 wins. He was 37 years old and pitched 380 innings. In 1989 Bret Saberhagen of Kansas City led the majors in innings pitched with 262⅓. Saberhagen was only 25, and he was dynamite—going 23–6, with a 2.16 ERA, and winning the Cy Young Award. But he finished only 12 of the 35 games he started.

Managers like the Royals' John Wathan have learned that even a Saberhagen often isn't as good a bet—late in a close game—as a fresh, skilled reliever like the Royals' Jeff Montgomery, who compiled 7 wins, 18 saves and a 1.37 ERA in 1989. That simple truth, which took decades to discover and more decades to really soak in, is that a rubber-armed pitcher with only one or two good pitches can kill the opposition for an inning or two. The same pitcher might be ordinary or worse as a starter; second or third time through the order, opposing hitters would have already measured that one outstanding pitch.

So why not use him as a specialist? Gradually, managers did. Joe Page's great pitch was a fastball, Elroy Face's was a forkball, Hoyt Wilhelm's was a knuckler, Sparky Lyle's was a slider and Bruce Sutter's was a split-finger

fastball. Lyle won the AL Cy Young Award in 1977, going 13–5 with 26 saves for the Yankees; he was dumped from his perch as top reliever in 1978 when the Yanks signed Goose Gossage, whose fastball was even harder to hit than Lyle's slider.

More refinements were still to come. Relief aces like Page, Face and Lyle won a lot of games because they were often brought in relatively early in a game. Casey Stengel, for one, believed in using his best pinch hitters whenever the opportunity for a big rally arose, even if it was in, say, the second inning. Stengel used his ace relievers much the same way. In the second-to-last game of the 1949 season, with the pennant on the line, Stengel brought in Joe Page in the third inning. The Red Sox were ahead, 2–0, and had the bases loaded with only one out. Page walked in two runs, but then he settled down and zipped his hummer past Ted Williams, Junior Stephens and the other Boston sluggers. He finished the game as the Yankees came from behind to win—and, the next day, to win again and nail down the pennant.

Gradually, managers began to nurture their ace closers like hothouse flowers. Today the conventional wisdom is to bring in the ace closer no earlier than the eighth inning, and only if the game is tied or if you lead by one or two runs. Don't waste your ace in a losing situation, and don't tire him. Some managers cut it even finer than that, rarely bringing in their ace before the ninth, and only to protect a lead. In 1989 Mitch Williams of the Cubs relieved in 76 games—he never started, of course—yet pitched only 81⅔ innings. He won four games and saved 36, and the Cubs won the NL East.

Every reliever needs a great pitch, and a fiery temperament doesn't hurt, either. The Cubs' Mitch Williams is known as "Wild Thing" for his personality, his follow-through and his lack of control. In 1989 he earned 36 saves but walked 52 batters in 81⅔ innings. In one outing he hit two batters in a row, threw a wild pitch, walked the pitcher and committed a balk—all in succession.

Continued on page 118

Billy Southworth

Billy Southworth is often described as one of John McGraw's disciples, but in fact Southworth hated the strict discipline enforced by McGraw. He preferred a much gentler managing style that not only won favor among players, but pennants as well. In 13 years as a major league manager, he won four pennants and two world championships.

Southworth had established himself as a fine defensive outfielder and a consistent .300 hitter by the time he was traded to the New York Giants in 1924. "Working for McGraw, a player ceased to be an individual," Southworth later said. "I was unable to subordinate myself to McGraw's rigid system. So when he decided in 1926 that I was, from his viewpoint, hopeless, he traded me."

The trade sent Southworth to the Cardinals, and on September 24 his two-run homer—against the Giants—clinched the 1926 pennant for St. Louis. In 1929 Southworth became the Cardinal manager. Branch Rickey, the team's general manager, advised him to be tough with his players, but the low-key Southworth couldn't bring the Cards any higher than fourth place, and Rickey demoted him to a minor league post. Southworth won consistently in the minors and returned to the Cardinal helm in 1940.

His timing was good. Rickey was putting together a superb roster, and in 1942 Southworth was blessed with a team that included rookie sluggers Stan Musial, Whitey Kurowski and Harry Walker, and rookie pitcher Johnny Beazley, who went 21–6. Enos Slaughter, Terry Moore and Marty Marion anchored the team, and seven Cardinal pitchers posted ERAs under 3.00. On August 15 the Cardinals trailed the Brooklyn Dodgers by 9½ games. Southworth kept his cool; his approach to players was firm, friendly and matter-of-fact, and the Cards

won 30 of their next 36 games—for a total of 106—to edge the Dodgers by two games.

The favored Yankees clubbed the Cardinals in the first game of the 1942 World Series, but St. Louis came back to win the next four games. Southworth's team coasted to pennants in 1943 and 1944, losing to the Yankees in the 1943 Series and then beating the St. Louis Browns in the "Streetcar Series" of 1944.

Although Southworth treated his players with respect, his fundamental strategy was in line with McGraw's. The Cardinals boasted strong pitching and defense, so Southworth frequently played for one run. Even Musial and Slaughter got the bunt sign—and complied. Rickey described Southworth as "the perfect manager—gentlemanly, shrewd and inspirational."

In 1946 Southworth pulled a surprise, leaving the successful Cardinals to manage the Boston Braves, who hadn't won a pennant since 1914. The Braves offered him more money, and he wanted a challenge. In 1948 Southworth coaxed an uncharacteristically strong effort from outfielder Jeff Heath, who hit .319 with 20 homers. Other Braves had fine seasons, but the team is best remembered for a rhyme that described its thin pitching staff —"Spahn, Sain, and two days of rain." Warren Spahn and Johnny Sain won 39 games between them, and the Braves took the pennant, only to lose the World Series to Cleveland.

Midway through the 1951 season, with his team in fifth place, Southworth retired. He was a rare manager, a nice guy who produced championship teams. Veteran shortstop Dick Bartell summed up Southworth's style: "He believed a kind word would get more out of a man than a snarl or a nasty crack."

BILLY SOUTHWORTH

Manager
St. Louis Cardinals 1929,
1940-1945
Boston Braves 1946-1951

GAMES	1,770
WINS	
Career	1,044
Season High	106
LOSSES	
Career	704
Season High	72
WINNING PERCENTAGE	
Career *(5th all time)*	.597
Season High *(10th all time)*	.688
PENNANTS	1942, 1943, 1944, 1948
WORLD CHAMPIONSHIPS	1942, 1944

According to shortstop Dick Bartell, Billy Southworth (left) was not only a good manager, but something of a humanitarian. "He believed that a kind word would get more out of a man than a snarl or a nasty crack," Bartell said. "He encouraged the guy who was down, and remembered that all players are human."

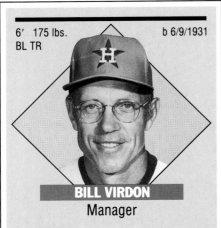

6' 175 lbs.   b 6/9/1931
BL TR

BILL VIRDON
Manager

Nobody's butt ever got too warm sitting on Bill Virdon's bench. Virdon, a big-league manager for 13 years, won three division titles largely by making the most of his 25-man roster.

After a 12-year career as a fine defensive center fielder, Virdon became manager of the Pirates in 1972, the year after they took the World Series. Virdon inherited sluggers like Willie Stargell and Roberto Clemente, but it was Virdon's masterful juggling of his bench and pitching staff that earned the Bucs another NL East title in 1972. Ten pitchers had at least 25 appearances as the Pirates posted a 2.81 team ERA.

But toward the end of the 1973 season the Pirates were hovering around .500, and Virdon was fired. He then spent a year and a half as the Yankees' manager. His forthright, low-key manner tested owner George Steinbrenner's patience, and Virdon was fired midway through the 1975 season. He was picked up almost immediately by Houston, where he remained through the 1982 season. Blessed with a fine pitching staff, Virdon's Astros won the NL West in 1980, and repeated in the second half of the 1981 split season.

But Virdon never came through in the postseason. His 1972 Pirates were three outs away from the World Series when the Reds scored twice in the ninth inning of Game 5 of the NLCS; his 1980 Astros led 5–2 in Game 5 before losing to the Phillies, 8–7; and his 1981 Astros blew a 2–0 lead in the best-of-five NL West playoffs against the Dodgers.

The relief ace on six Yankee pennant winners from 1936 to 1943, Johnny "Fireman" Murphy was the best of his era. When starter Lefty Gomez was asked how many games he'd win, his stock reply was, "I dunno. Ask Murphy."

As the "closer" specialty became more rarefied, other pitching specialties were gradually created. To get to the point where he can use his closer, a manager today needs middle relievers and setup men he can bring in as early as the fifth or sixth inning, even if the starter has been pitching well. Mark Williamson of the Orioles rarely appears early in a game, but he's ready in the sixth or seventh inning to set up Baltimore's closer, Gregg Olson.

Much of this refinement comes from the increasing use of player-against-player data. Statistics prove that a right-handed pitcher has an advantage over a right-handed batter, and a lefty against a left-handed batter. So if his pitching staff is less than overpowering—and almost every pitching staff is—it makes sense for a manager to use that advantage all he can. It even makes sense for teams with a great closer, like the 1988 AL champion Oakland Athletics. The A's had baseball's finest closer in right-handed sinker-baller Dennis Eckersley, who saved 45 games. But Eckersley's job—and manager Tony LaRussa's—was made easier by a fine, well-balanced stable of set-up men. Right-handed relievers Gene Nelson and Eric Plunk combined with lefties Rick Honeycutt and Greg Cadaret for a 22-12 record and 18 saves for Oakland, and their work enabled LaRussa to reserve Eckersley for the all-important ninth inning. The A's won 104 games, and led the majors with 64 saves.

Everyone knows that right-handed pitchers generally do better against right-handed batters, but managers nowadays are armed with statistics telling them much more. Paul Molitor of the Milwaukee Brewers bats right-handed, but hits righties better than lefties, so you go against the book on him. Dan Pasqua of the White Sox is helpless against left-handed

pitchers. Jose Canseco of the Oakland A's has trouble hitting journeyman Dave LaPoint, of all people, but kills Toronto ace Jimmy Key. Twice in 1989, the Cardinals issued intentional walks to get to the Mets' left-handed slugger Darryl Strawberry—who was easy meat for the Cards' southpaw relief ace, Ken Dayley. If you were a manager, you would be dumb not to use that kind of information. The more you use it, the more you relieve, and the more specialized your pitchers become.

While relief pitchers have gone one way, often depending on just a great fastball or slider or split-finger, starters have gone the other. The major leagues used to be full of pitchers who threw a fastball only, or a fastball and a curve. Some were great; in their prime, Walter Johnson and Lefty Grove threw nothing but fastballs, and they are generally regarded to be among the greatest pitchers in history. But Johnson and Grove were exceptions. As the hitting explosion rocked baseball in the 1920s, many pitchers found themselves unable to cope.

Today it is hard to imagine a pitcher not throwing his hardest. But that is what pitchers used to do. Christy Mathewson, who starred for the New York Giants from 1900 through 1916, was a master at "pacing himself," as it was called. The ball was so dead that, for the most part, a pitcher didn't need to worry about game-winning homers; a well-hit ball was much more likely to put runners on first and third. Anyway, the pitcher was supposed to still be strong in the ninth inning—and beyond, if need be. So a starter saved his strength for crucial situations.

Still, once home runs became more frequent, pitching took a long time to catch up. Listen to Paul Richards, a major league catcher of the 1930s and 1940s and a manager, coach and general manager through the 1950s,

The bullpen became the home of baseball's emerging stars in the 1970s, as one-pitch wonders with engaging personalities eclipsed starters as fan favorites. When Al "the Mad Hungarian" Hrabosky didn't get named to the All-Star team in 1974, St. Louis fans responded with "We Hlove Hrabosky Hbanner Hday" (above).

Even a star like Boston's Roger Clemens (right) has to chart pitches the day before a start. The chart details the type, location and ultimate destination of each pitch.

In 1950 Del Ennis hit .311 with 31 homers and a league-high 126 RBI for the NL champion Phillies, but it was his teammate, palmball artist Jim Konstanty (above), who was named MVP. It was the first time a reliever won the award, and Konstanty outpolled runner-up Stan Musial by almost two to one.

1960s and most of the 1970s: "Pitchers are much better than they used to be. The oldtimers only remember the outstanding ones. They forget about the soft touches who couldn't hold a job today. Let's go back to the 1930s, and that means we're actually talking about the modern era. Most of the pitchers threw a fastball and curve. That was it. There were some cute ones around, too, but they weren't the stars. Even some of the stars had a curve that was nothing special and today they couldn't make it with just the pitches they had."

Pitchers needed new weapons—new pitches—and gradually they developed them. The slider was developed about 1930—George Blaeholder of the St. Louis Browns usually gets the inventor's credit—but it took a long time for pitchers to assimilate it and to realize how important it is to use a variety of pitches. Don Drysdale, a great Dodger pitcher of the 1950s and 1960s and later a baseball broadcaster, said: "What you're trying to do as a pitcher is to keep the hitter off balance. Don't let him get that same stride, that same motion, that grooved swing all the time, as a golfer would. You want to back them off the plate. You want to change speeds. That's why the slider, when it came into existence, gave Williams and Musial so damned much trouble. They could gauge the speed of the fastball. Now all of a sudden the slider comes to be a dominant pitch. It is thrown harder than the curve ball, and just a shade slower than the fastball, yet it has a little break to it. Here's a whole new thing coming in! Stan told me he used to sit and watch a pitcher, and his computer mind would think, 'What is the speed of his best fastball? What is the speed of anything else he throws—curve ball, or change?' Now he has to work in the slider. There's a new element in there."

The slider helped a lot, but so did the growing use of spitballs and other

such illegal pitches, thrown by anywhere from 10 to 50 percent of today's pitchers, depending upon whose estimate you prefer. In the late 1970s another dazzling new pitch appeared: the split-finger fastball, a superior cousin of the old forkball. Bruce Sutter threw a hard split-finger that seemed to dive under bats. Pitching for the Cubs and then the Cardinals, he led the NL in saves five times. Sutter shares inventor's credit with Roger Craig, one-time pitching coach for Detroit, San Diego and Houston, and manager of the San Francisco Giants. Craig taught the split-finger to every pitcher in sight, on his team and others, and it spread through baseball quickly. Mike Scott of the Houston Astros picked it up and promptly went from 5–11, 4.68 in 1984, to 18–8, 3.29 in 1985; in 1986 he went 18–10, 2.22, and won the Cy Young Award.

Jim Bouton earned the nickname "Bulldog" for his ferocious fastball and gung-ho attitude with the Yankees in the 1960s. But an arm injury forced him to turn to the knuckleball —and middle relief, one of the bottom rungs on the pitching ladder—in 1969. Despite a total of 73 appearances that season with Seattle and Houston, Bouton had a 2–3 record and two saves.

Strategy is just as important to the care and management of the starting rotation as it is to use of relief pitchers. Again, statistics help; managers juggle their rotations to protect a pitcher from a team that tends to rack him, and to give him an extra start against a team he often beats. When Earl Weaver was managing the Orioles, he kept a rotation calendar a month ahead and juggled it to take advantage of matchups or for other strategic reasons. "During the season, a manager doesn't do much that's brilliant," Weaver told writer Tom Boswell. Tapping his rotation calendar, he added: "Sometimes I think about the only way I might win a couple of extra ones for us is right here."

For all the changes in pitching and pitching strategy, much remains the same. Good starters mix up their pitches, but most pitchers throw the fastball at least three pitches out of five. That may sound crude and unscientific,

Best in the Pen

The effectiveness of relief pitching is perhaps the single most influential change in baseball over the years. Relief pitchers have now become so effective that it takes a near-superhuman season to get noticed. From Firpo Marberry to Dennis Eckersley, great relief performances have carried teams to many a pennant and World Series. Below are some of the best:

Name	Year	G	IP	W–L	ERA	SV	BB	SO
Firpo Marberry, WAS	1926	64	138	12-7	3.00	22	66	43
● Joe Page, NY (AL)	1949	60	135$\frac{1}{3}$	13-8	2.59	27	75	99
● Jim Konstanty, PHI (AL)	1950	74	152	16-7	2.66	22	50	56
Roy Face, PIT	1959	57	93$\frac{1}{3}$	18-1	2.70	10	25	69
● Ron Perranoski, LA	1963	69	129	16-3	1.67	21	43	75
Hoyt Wilhelm, CHI (AL)	1964	73	131$\frac{1}{3}$	12-9	1.99	27	30	95
● Phil Regan, LA	1966	65	116$\frac{2}{3}$	14-1	1.62	21	24	88
John Hiller, DET	1973	65	125	10-5	1.44	38	39	124
● Mike Marshall, LA	1974	106	208	15-12	2.42	21	56	143
Goose Gossage, PIT	1977	72	133	11-9	1.62	26	49	151
● Rollie Fingers, MIL	1981	47	78	6-3	1.04	28	13	61
Dan Quisenberry, KC	1983	69	139	5-3	1.94	45	11	48
Bruce Sutter, StL	1984	71	122$\frac{2}{3}$	5-7	1.54	45	23	77
Dave Righetti, NY (AL)	1986	74	106$\frac{2}{3}$	8-8	2.45	46	35	83
● Dennis Eckersley, OAK	1989	51	57	4-0	1.56	33	3	55
● Mark Davis, SD	1989	70	92$\frac{2}{3}$	4-3	1.85	44	31	92

● team won division title
● team won pennant
● team won World Series

but Satchel Paige used to call his fastball his "thoughtful stuff," because it gave hitters so much to think about. As for the alleged changes in pitching conditions, Paige once observed that "home plate don't move."

If you listen to television commentary by Tom Seaver, Jim Palmer and Tim McCarver, you know that effective pitching combines raw speed, variety, control and intelligence. Onetime students of pitching, Seaver and Palmer graduated to become professors of the craft. Both had outstanding fastballs —an endowed skill—and both learned to mix their hummers with breaking balls and off-speed pitches, moving the ball around in and near the strike zone. More of that goes on now: young pitchers learn refinements in college ball before they even come near the majors. And there is also more talk of intelligence in pitching, though it is doubtful that modern pitchers are any smarter than their forebears. For the view of an old-timer, look back to Kirby Higbe, an ace left-hander for the Brooklyn Dodgers of the 1940s. "I'll tell you what my philosophy was when I was pitching," Higbe said. "I never tried to outsmart a hitter. I always tried to out-dummy them." ⚾

A reliever's life is an uncertain one. In 1986 sinkerballer Roger McDowell (opposite) posted 14 wins and 22 saves for the world champion New York Mets, but he became expendable when Randy Myers emerged as the bullpen ace. A team has only enough room for one closer, so in 1989 McDowell was traded to Philadelphia, where he earned 19 saves for manager Jim Leyva.

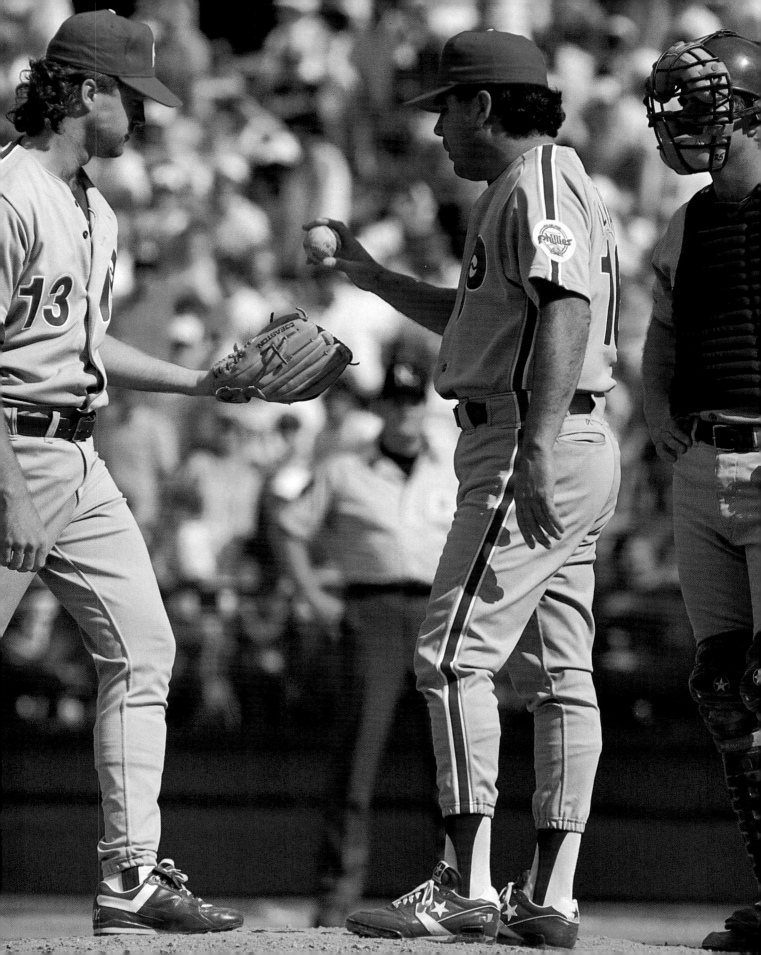

Wilbert Robinson

He played in *three* major leagues, caught for the championship Baltimore Orioles of the 1890s, became a great pitching coach and managed the Brooklyn Dodgers to two pennants. Yet Wilbert Robinson is best remembered as "Uncle Robbie," the indulgent manager of Brooklyn's Daffiness Boys, and the butt of one of Casey Stengel's funniest practical jokes.

The Dodgers were training at Daytona Beach, Florida, in 1916, Robinson's third year at the helm. One day, he and several of his players were watching a publicity stunt in which a sporting goods representative dropped golf balls from an airplane 1,000 feet above the beach. The balls hit hard, boring into the sand, but the old catcher was not intimidated.

"I bet I could catch a baseball if somebody threw one out of that airplane for me," Robinson said. His players warned that he might be killed, but Robinson scoffed. "I never got hit on the head with a ball in my life," he said. The stunt was arranged for the next day. A Brooklyn trainer was to drop the ball from the plane, but Stengel, the Dodger right fielder, slipped him a grapefruit instead.

The sphere dropped from 400 feet. Robinson, by then a rotund 52-year-old, circled under it and set himself for the catch. But the grapefruit was falling fast. It zoomed through his hands and exploded on his chest, knocking him down and drenching him with juice. "Jesus!" he wailed. "I'm killed! I'm blind! It's broke open my chest! I'm covered with blood!" Robinson's players howled. The embarrassed manager threatened to release Stengel. Characteristically, however, he soon cooled off. "Pretty good," he said. "I must have looked like a damned fool."

Though long on baseball knowledge, Robinson was short on education. Writing out his lineup one day, he found himself unable to spell the name of outfielder Otto Roettger. "Oh hell," he said in frustration. "Maybe I should start Dick Cox." Roettger sat that day; Cox played.

Robinson was a fine catcher with a strong arm. He played from 1886 through 1902, a period when baseball was in transition, but spent most of his career with the Baltimore Orioles. The Orioles were a rowdy, scrappy bunch, winning pennants in 1894, 1895 and 1896. Robinson and John McGraw were teammates, and when McGraw was managing the New York Giants he hired Robinson as a coach in 1911. The old catcher became one of baseball's first and best pitching coaches, polishing Rube Marquard and Jeff Tesreau into aces as the Giants won pennants in 1911, 1912 and 1913. But he and McGraw were polar opposites. McGraw was a stern, angry disciplinarian who called every play and almost every pitch, while Robinson was cheerful and easygoing. They had a falling-out over a missed signal in the 1913 World Series and didn't speak to each other for years.

The Dodgers hired Robinson as manager in 1914. McGraw gave up on Marquard, and Connie Mack, manager of the Philadelphia Athletics, gave up on Jack Coombs, one of his aces. Robinson grabbed them both, revived them and won the pennant in 1916. He won another pennant in 1920, and he came close in 1924 and again in 1930.

Mixed in were lots of years in the second division, but Robinson's style and personality made him a beloved figure in Brooklyn, win or lose. He walked home from Ebbets Field arguing cheerfully with fans

No man ever managed the Dodgers as long—or as affectionately—as Wilbert Robinson. Once Robinson hugged a runner as he rounded third, causing him to be thrown out at home.

about his team, his players and his strategy—or lack thereof. While Robinson was at the helm, the Brooklyn team was affectionately known as "the Robins."

Brooklyn players had it easy. They could—and did—read newspapers in the dugout. The Robins were rallying one day when infielder Chick Fewster started pounding a bat on the dugout steps. "Cut that out!" yelled Robinson. He pointed to pitcher Jess Petty, who was asleep at the end of the bench. "I don't want you to disturb old Jess."

But bad luck seemed to dog Robinson's teams. In New York, they played third fiddle to the Giants and Yankees, and sometimes nothing would go right for them. Robinson believed in sticking with his starting pitchers, and on Saturday, May 1, 1920, at Braves Field, he stuck with Leon Cadore for 26 innings. Boston manager George Stallings let Joe Oeschger pitch 26 innings, too. The game was called on account of darkness, with the score 1–1.

Sunday baseball was illegal in Boston, so that night Brooklyn took a midnight train ride home, where they lost to the Phillies on Sunday, 4–3, in 13 innings. Back to Boston rode the weary team for a Monday game with the Braves, who won, 2–1, in 19 innings. Brooklyn had played 58 innings in three days without a win.

Robinson liked big pitchers who could throw hard. Dazzy Vance, 6' 2" and 200 pounds, flunked trials with the Pirates and the Yankees, but not with Robinson, who took him on as a 31-year-old rookie in 1922. Vance threw one of history's greatest fastballs, and with Robinson's help he harnessed it, leading the NL in strikeouts seven straight years and winning 20 or more games three times.

Robinson was a modest manager. He knew the season was long and one man's judgment was often as good as another's. He sometimes let sportswriters fill out the lineup. In 1930 Robinson had a team that he described as his best. Vance was still overpowering, and the lineup featured Babe Herman, the daffiest of the Daffiness Boys but a slugger who hit .393 that year with 35 homers and 130 RBI.

Brooklyn led the NL most of the season, but lost four straight and went into a July 4 game with a lead of one percentage point. Robinson let Herman pick the batting order. Herman asked his teammates where they wanted to bat, filled requests as best he could and watched with pleasure as they won.

They almost won the 1930 pennant, but fell short in a four-team race and finished fourth. They finished fourth again in 1931, and Robinson was fired. He retired to his home in Georgia, but then was hired as manager and president of the Atlanta team of the Southern Association. Atlanta fans loved to watch the rotund old gent in the dugout, chewing tobacco, eating watermelon and otherwise enjoying the game.

He left behind a 19-year managing career in which he won just one more game than he lost, but the ex-catcher helped give the game some of its finest pitchers, among them Hall of Famer Burleigh Grimes. Grimes went from 3–16 with Pittsburgh in 1918 to 19–9 with Brooklyn in 1919, and his ERA dropped from 3.53 to 2.14. "Robinson was the guy who made a pitcher out of me," he said.

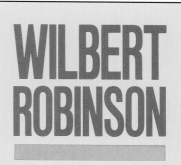

WILBERT ROBINSON

Manager
Baltimore Orioles 1902
Brooklyn Dodgers 1914-1931
Hall of Fame 1945

GAMES	2,819
WINS	
Career	1,399
Season High	94
LOSSES	
Career	1,398
Season High	88
WINNING PERCENTAGE	
Career	.500
Season High	.610
PENNANTS	1916, 1920

John McGraw (opposite, left) was Robinson's teammate on the Baltimore Orioles and later his boss on the New York Giants. Among other things, Robinson was responsible for placating umpires whom McGraw had enraged. "Robinson was the sugar, I was the vinegar," McGraw said.

Whiteyball

t's hard to steal a pennant, but once every couple of decades a team
wins for reasons no one can quite figure out. The 1987 St. Louis Cardinals were such a team, and their manager, Whitey Herzog, was
widely credited with a managerial tour de force. Herzog deserved the
credit, but he didn't win that pennant with smoke and mirrors. He won
it with personnel and strategy geared to benefit from defense, speed and relief pitching. Together, those elements made up what Cardinal fans called
"Whiteyball." It was fun to watch, it drove opposing teams crazy and under
Herzog's direction it produced six division championships in 12 years: three
straight for the Kansas City Royals from 1976 to 1978, and three more for the
Cardinals in 1982, 1985 and 1987.

The St. Louis team of 1987 was the most improbable winner among the
six. Some thought a rabbit ball was in play that season, because never before
had so many home runs hopped over the fences. Both leagues set homer
records—the American League with 2,634; the National with 1,824. An
even 100 grand slams were hit—another record. Detroit won the AL East
championship and hit 225 homers; Minnesota won the West and hit 196. San
Francisco won the NL West with 205 yet St. Louis took the East with a mere
94. No other team in the majors had fewer than 100 homers; 11 of the 26
big-league clubs out-homered the Cards by more than 2 to 1.

The Cards had one big slugger in first baseman Jack Clark, who hit 35
homers and drove in 106 runs. But on September 9, with the Cards already
slumping and their lead cut to a game and a half, Clark sprained his ankle and
was lost for the season. It looked like a death blow, because the team was already riddled with injuries. Pitcher John Tudor was sidelined with a broken
leg, suffered when Barry Lyons, a catcher for the New York Mets, fell on

First baseman Jack Clark was Herzog's designated power hitter in the mid-1980s, but being the only slugger in the lineup made him pretty easy to pitch around. In 1987 he managed 35 home runs, but was walked 136 times, the most since Willie McCovey's 137 in 1970.

Once Herzog installed Frank White as the Royals' regular second baseman in 1975, he stopped worrying about second base. "I've never seen a second baseman with the range he has," Herzog said of the eight-time Gold Glove winner.

Tudor's leg while chasing a pop foul into the Cardinal dugout. Danny Cox, the Cards' best right-handed starter, was hit by a line drive on July 9 and missed a month. Tony Pena, a star catcher acquired from Pittsburgh, missed six weeks with a broken thumb; Tommy Herr, the veteran second baseman who batted third in the lineup, was out for three weeks with a muscle injury.

So the Cardinals didn't win with power or with the usual kind of pitching —no one on the staff won more than 11 games. The New York Mets had injuries of their own but should have won the division easily. Their pitching was strong, with a division-low ERA of 3.84, and their slugging was fearsome: 39 homers for Darryl Strawberry, 36 for Howard Johnson, 29 for Kevin McReynolds, 20 for Gary Carter. The Mets led the league in runs scored with 823 and in hits with 1,499.

So how did the Cardinals win? Herzog urged them to hit the ball on the ground, to bunt when the need arose, to run and steal bases whenever they could. They stole at least 200 bases every year for seven straight seasons—a feat unequaled since the first two decades of this century. In 1987 the Cards stole 248 bases, tops in the majors. Vince Coleman, the leadoff man and left fielder, led the league with 109, and shortstop Ozzie Smith had 43. With the exception of Clark, everyone in the lineup could run, and did. Cardinal baserunners continually went for the extra base, and the threat posed by Coleman, Smith, Willie McGee and other speedsters unnerved opposing pitchers, catchers and infielders, prompting misplays that yielded more bases, and more runs. Jim Frey, manager and then general manager of the Cubs, said this of Coleman: "You look around and he's up at bat and the other team has got the third baseman playing in, the second baseman is in by two full strides, and the first baseman's up on the grass. You got no choice." De-

Speedster Vince Coleman probably slid back into first base more often than he slid into second in the late 1980s, as pitchers tried to wear him out with pickoff throws. It didn't work, however, as Coleman ignited Herzog's Cardinals to pennants in 1985 and 1987, stealing 110 and 109 bases, respectively.

spite their lack of power and their ordinary team batting average of .263, the Cards scored 798 runs, second in the NL only to the Mets.

Yet runs weren't the only payoff from Cardinal speed, and may not have been the biggest. "Speed probably is more important to us on defense," Herzog said. "People overlook that." People overlook a lot about defense, which, over the years, has probably improved more than any other part of the game. With bigger gloves, fielders can make catches impossible in past generations. Charlie Gehringer, the Detroit Tigers' star second baseman from 1926 through 1942, tips his cap to the fielders of today. "I've seen plays I can't believe, infield and outfield," he said. "The equipment's made a tremendous difference. They make plays now on balls we could knock down but couldn't keep in the glove. The infields are smoother. They level out the infield at the five-inning mark. Didn't do that in our day."

In addition, today's ballparks are bigger, particularly in the NL. Herzog was among the first to realize that big, lumbering outfielders—tolerated in earlier days, if they could hit—would fare poorly in the vast outfield reaches of St. Louis' Busch Stadium and other modern ballparks. He went instead for fast outfielders who could chase down fly balls and cut off liners in the gaps. "I tell our pitchers that in the big National League parks, with the greatest defense in baseball behind them, all they need to do is to move the ball around, throw strikes, and let McGee, Coleman and Andy Van Slyke run down their mistakes," Herzog wrote in his autobiography.

So much for the Cardinal outfield, which Herzog rated as the best in baseball history. Van Slyke went to Pittsburgh in the trade for Pena, but his replacements—Curt Ford, John Morris and, later, Tom Brunansky—also

fielded well. The Cardinal infield was just as good. Ozzie Smith is generally considered to be the best defensive shortstop in history—at the most important defensive position. Terry Pendleton, at third, was almost as good, and so was Herr, at second. The Cardinals led the NL in fielding percentage in 1987 for the fourth straight year. They also did it in 1988 and 1989.

But the Cards were even better than their statistics indicated. They were anything but cautious: Smith, Pendleton, Herr, McGee and Coleman sprinted and dived for anything remotely within reach, and came up throwing. They risked errors, yet made fewer than other teams. Herzog estimated that Smith alone saved 100 runs a year with his spectacular play at shortstop.

If Herzog's offensive strategy sounds like John McGraw's, Herzog isn't ashamed of the comparison. In another important area of the game, however, his strategy was as modern as a space probe. He used his bullpen as artfully as any manager in baseball. Herzog often used as many as five or six pitchers in a low-scoring game, switching from a lefty to a righty when a right-handed hitter came up in a threatening situation, going to another southpaw when a left-handed batter came up and finally bringing in his big closer.

Doubling as general manager, Herzog moved heaven and earth between the 1980 and 1981 seasons to get a strong bullpen closer. He came up with the two best in baseball: right-handers Rollie Fingers and Bruce Sutter. Since he had room for only one right-handed closer, Herzog traded Fingers to the Milwaukee Brewers. Sutter won nine games for the Cards in 1982 and saved 36. He did just as well as St. Louis swept Atlanta in the NLCS and then edged Milwaukee four games to three in the World Series.

Herzog credited Sutter for that pennant and world championship. But by 1985 Sutter was pitching for Atlanta. Herzog reverted to a "bullpen by

Outfielder David Green was the key to a major trade made by Herzog with the Royals in 1982, but personal problems—including his fear for his family's safety in Nicaragua—kept him from realizing his potential. Green (left) was another of Whitey's speedy outfielders, and in 1983 he had his best season, hitting .284 with 34 stolen bases.

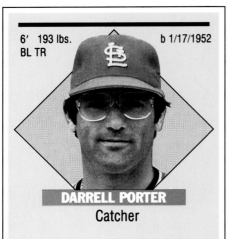

6' 193 lbs.
BL TR

b 1/17/1952

DARRELL PORTER
Catcher

It was a gamble and Whitey Herzog knew it. Darrell Porter had been one of baseball's most productive catchers in the 1970s. In 1973, at 21, Porter became the Milwaukee Brewers' regular catcher, hitting a respectable .254. And when he joined manager Herzog at Kansas City, his reputation grew. In 1979 he became only the second catcher in major league history to top 100 in runs scored, with 101; RBI, with 112; and walks, with a league-leading 121. Herzog called the four-time All-Star "the best in the league."

But Porter missed part of the 1980 season in treatment for drug and alcohol abuse. He claimed the treatment was successful, became a free agent in 1981 and said he was ready to play.

Herzog, managing the St. Louis Cardinals, took a chance. "I wanted Porter a lot," he said. "He'd been a fiery guy, a leader, a guy who handled pitchers well, and he threw well enough to keep baserunners honest on the rug. I was sure that if he said he was OK, he was OK." And though the Cards' new catcher did fine behind the plate in 1981 and 1982, he hit just .224 and .231, respectively.

But the Cards won the NL East in 1982, and Porter came alive in the postseason. He hit an amazing .556 in the NL Championship Series as the Cards swept the Braves. And with timely hitting and outstanding defense, he took MVP honors in the Cards' 4–3 World Series victory over the Brewers. The gamble had paid off.

Terry Pendleton's debut at third base in 1984 gave Herzog four switch-hitters in his lineup, making it nearly impossible for the opposition to play the percentages when bringing in relievers. Pendleton's speed and defense didn't hurt, either.

committee," with right-hander Jeff Lahti saving 19 games, left-hander Ken Dayley saving 11 and rookie right-hander Todd Worrell coming up late in the season to win 3 and save 5. In 1987 Worrell won 8 games and saved 33.

As much as Herzog depended on great relievers like Sutter and Worrell, he also coaxed valuable contributions from Dayley, a short reliever with a live fastball, and from an ever-changing list of no-name middle relievers. Still, Herzog, like any manager, was delighted when a starter pitched well enough to go all the way. His 1985 champions had strong starters, with John Tudor, who went 21–8, pitching 14 complete games, and Joaquin Andujar and Danny Cox, who went 21–12 and 18–9, pitching ten each.

But the 1987 Cardinal starters were so riddled with injuries and so inconsistent when they did pitch that Herzog had to use his bullpen early and often. Rookie Joe Magrane, 9–7, led the team in complete games with four; the whole Cardinal pitching staff threw only ten complete games. Yet Herzog was able to win by shuttling in guys like Bill Dawley, Pat Perry, Lee Tunnell, Steve Peters and Ricky Horton, all before getting to his bullpen aces, Worrell and Dayley. "Nowadays," said Herzog, "it's what baseball is all about: whether my bullpen can out-do yours. If you don't have outstanding relief pitching, you might as well piss on the fire and call in the dogs."

Herzog's bullpen strategy dovetailed neatly with his bench strategy. More than other managers, he somehow arranged to get the lefty-righty advantage both ways: by juggling his lineup and bullpen, he could get the best out of his southpaw pitchers against the other team's left-handed hitters, his right-handed pitchers against right-handed hitters, his left-handed hitters against *right-handed* pitchers, his right-

With talent like Milt Thompson on the bench, Herzog didn't have to panic if one of his starters went down with an injury. When Cards center fielder Willie McGee was hurt in 1989, Thompson filled in admirably, hitting .290 and stealing 27 bases.

At 5'5" and 148 pounds, Freddie Patek was baseball's smallest player in the 1970s. But in addition to being one of the game's best base-stealers, he was nimble and tough enough to lead AL shortstops in double plays his first four seasons in the majors, 1971 to 1974.

handed hitters against the other team's southpaws. Herzog was a master of the double switch. For example, let's say the game is tied, the Mets are threatening in the last of the eighth and Herzog wants to bring in a reliever. The Cardinal pitcher is due to lead off the next inning. In addition to the reliever, Herzog brings in a new right fielder. He puts the right fielder in the lineup's ninth slot—enabling him to lead off the Cardinal ninth—and the pitcher bat's in the right-fielder's spot.

Like Earl Weaver, Herzog also kept track of individual matchups. In the 1987 NLCS, the Cardinals trailed the San Francisco Giants, three games to two. St. Louis led the sixth game, 1–0, going into the ninth; Worrell had relieved Tudor and was pitching well. He struck out Will Clark to lead off the Giant ninth. Roger Craig sent up Harry Spilman, a lefty, to pinch-hit, and Herzog remembered that Spilman had homered off Worrell earlier that season. So Herzog brought in Dayley, the left-hander. To keep his options open, he moved Worrell to right field—a tactic borrowed from schoolboy baseball. Dayley closed out the game, and the Cards won the Series the next night, riding Cox's pitching to a 6–0 victory.

Part of Herzog's righty-lefty edge was achieved through the Cardinal organization's emphasis on switch-hitting. The Cardinal lineup of 1985 and 1987 featured five switch-hitters: Coleman, Smith, McGee, Pendleton and Herr. They often occupied five of the six top spots in the lineup, the switch-hitting parade leavened only by cleanup man Jack Clark, who batted right but could hit right-handed pitching. Opposing managers were often frustrated; how could they use their bullpens effectively against a lineup that could just turn around and bat the other way?

In the 1985 NLCS, Tommy Lasorda, manager of the Los Angeles

Continued on page 138

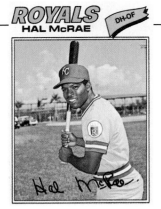

Hal McRae

Hal McRae played baseball as if it owed him money. His career was a nonstop, full-frontal assault on the game. Along the way he took a position nobody wanted—designated hitter—and turned it into a primary weapon on one of his era's finest teams—the Kansas City Royals.

But McRae's aggressive style of play nearly finished his major league career before it got started. After a 17-game stint as a rookie second baseman with Cincinnati in 1968, McRae was playing winter ball in Puerto Rico. He tried to score from third on a grounder, and the resulting collision at home plate left his right leg broken in four places. "I've sort of been an aggressive person all my life," he once said.

McRae missed the 1969 season, and when he came back he was switched to the outfield. His bat was still solid, but his lack of mobility limited his playing time with the talent-laden Big Red Machine. He played in two World Series with the Reds and averaged .450, but riding the pine and collecting postseason checks didn't sit well with a player of McRae's intensity.

In 1973 he got a break—in stereo. He was traded by the Reds to the Kansas City Royals, a young expansion team that needed a powerful bat in the lineup. And his arrival in the American League coincided with that of the designated hitter—the position McRae seemed born to play. But he tried to do too much at first. "I had been told in the National League that the American League was easy, so I felt I was going to come and just tear the league apart," he said. "I was going to hit home runs. As it turned out, I didn't hit anything. I fell on my face." McRae hit a career-low .234 that season with just nine home runs, but he was lucky. He happened to wear the same uniform as Charlie Lau, one of the game's finest hitting instructors. Lau helped him to relax at the plate and to hit to all fields. From then on McRae was a gap-hitting terror.

McRae put together a string of three straight .300-plus seasons, culminating with a .332 mark in 1976—just one point behind teammate and AL batting champ George Brett. But the Royals, managed by Whitey Herzog, won their first of three straight AL West titles, and McRae was the leading practitioner of Herzog's run-and-gun offense. In 1977 McRae laced 54 doubles, the most since George Kell's 56 in 1950, and a total that hasn't been equaled since. Then, in the ALCS against the Yankees, McRae made a play so aggressive he got his name in the rulebook. In Game 2, while trying to break up a double play, McRae threw a cross-body block on second baseman Willie Randolph, then held Randolph down and motioned Freddie Patek to score from third. The following spring the "McRae Rule" was routinely enforced, allowing umpires to call an automatic double play if a runner goes out of his way to upend an infielder making the pivot.

McRae continued to terrorize AL pitchers into the 1980s, and in 1982—at 37—he led the AL with 46 doubles and a club-record 133 RBI. His clutch hitting earned him the nickname "Mr. Ribbie," and his style of play earned the loyalty of his teammates and the enmity of his opponents. "He plays the game like everybody played it 25 years ago and, to me, that's just the way the game should be played," Herzog said. Even Seattle pitcher Glenn Abbott gave McRae a grudging compliment. "Over the years I feel McRae has played dirty, but he plays to win, and that's what it's all about."

Despite stars like George Brett and Frank White on the Royals in the late 1970s, Hal McRae's talent and aggressive style made him the undisputed team leader. "When Mac talks, I listen," Brett said. "He's the one that makes us go."

HAL McRAE

Designated Hitter
Cincinnati Reds 1968, 1970-1972
Kansas City Royals 1973-1987

GAMES	**2,084**
AT-BATS	**7,218**
BATTING AVERAGE	
Career	**.290**
Season High	**.332**
SLUGGING AVERAGE	
Career	**.454**
Season High	**.542**
HITS	
Career	**2,091**
Season High	**191**
DOUBLES	
Career	**484**
Season High	**54**
TRIPLES	
Career	**66**
Season High	**11**
HOME RUNS	
Career	**191**
Season High	**27**
RBI	
Career	**1,097**
Season High	**133**
RUNS	
Career	**940**
Season High	**104**
WORLD SERIES	**1970, 1972, 1980, 1985**

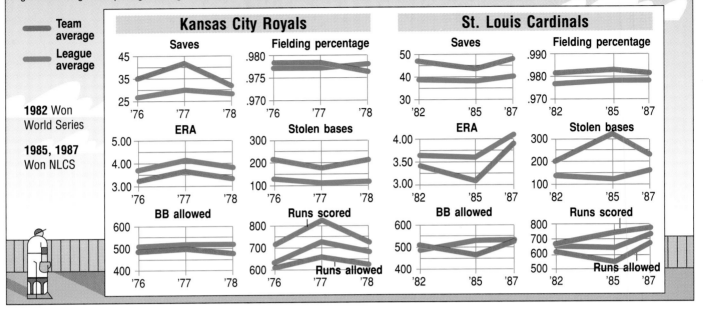

Beating the Averages

Whitey Herzog built his teams to win on the great plains of the Midwest — the great plains being the carpeted stadiums of Kansas City and St. Louis — and that means speed, strong pitching and good fielding. Comparing Herzog's teams' averages with league averages, ERAs are low, stolen bases high and only once in six division-winning years did his team lead the league in runs scored. Below is a look at Herzog's six division winners, and how their stats matched up with the league average.

— Team average
— League average

1982 Won World Series

1985, 1987 Won NLCS

Kansas City Royals

Saves
Fielding percentage
ERA
Stolen bases
BB allowed
Runs scored
Runs allowed

St. Louis Cardinals

Saves
Fielding percentage
ERA
Stolen bases
BB allowed
Runs scored
Runs allowed

If the mark of a great reliever is being at his best when the games are the biggest, then Ken Dayley qualifies. The Cardinal southpaw pitched a total of 20⅔ innings in postseason play in 1985 and 1987. He gave up one run, six hits and struck out 15 for an 0.44 ERA.

Dodgers, had a rare opportunity to use a righty-versus-righty advantage and lived to regret it. In Game 5 Ozzie Smith had used his switch-hitting skills to shock the Dodgers with a ninth-inning homer off Tom Niedenfuer, L.A.'s right-handed bullpen closer. It was the first homer Smith ever hit left-handed in more than 4,000 career at-bats, and it won the game, 3–2.

That put St. Louis up, three games to two. In Game 6, the Dodgers led, 5–4, with two out in the Cardinal ninth and runners on second and third. Niedenfuer was pitching. Clark, the right-hander, came to bat, with Van Slyke, a left-hander, on deck. Lasorda could have walked Clark. But after all, he reasoned, he had a good right-hander pitching. Why not use the edge? Niedenfuer threw a fastball, and Clark hit it 450 feet into the left field bleachers, giving St. Louis a 7–5 win and a four-games-to-two NLCS victory. "I was really glad to see them not walk me," Clark said. Niedenfuer was equally blunt. "The only way that shot would have stayed in the ballpark is if it hit the Goodyear blimp," he said.

The dramatic homers by Smith and Clark won that Series, but the Cards wouldn't have gone that far without old-fashioned Whiteyball. The Dodgers won the first two games. In the first inning of Game 3, Coleman singled and stole second. McGee walked. Bob Welch, the Dodger pitcher, threw wild, trying to pick Coleman off second. Coleman scored and McGee went to third—both runners gaining *two* bases on the errant throw. Herr walked and stole second. Pendleton drove in McGee with a grounder. In the second, Coleman walked, went to third on a bad pickoff throw by L.A. catcher Steve Scioscia and scored on a single by McGee.

Pendleton protected the Cardinal lead with a dazzling catch of a deep foul pop in the eighth and a backhanded stab of a smash in the ninth. As for

big-inning baseball, Whitey-style, look at the second inning of Game 4, when the Cards scored nine runs without an extra-base hit. Those two wins set up the home run dramatics by Smith and Clark.

Those homers were dramatic, but they almost obscured the Cards' usual way of scoring. In 1985, Tom Herr, batting third, drove in 110 runs while hitting only eight homers. In 1982 Keith Hernandez batted third, hit only seven homers and drove in 94 runs. In 1987 Smith batted second, didn't hit a single homer, yet drove in 75 runs, while Herr, batting third and managing only two homers, drove in 83. Herzog's strategy demonstrates that a team of speedy singles hitters can compete with a power club.

With Andy Van Slyke (18), Willie McGee (left) and Vince Coleman in the Cardinal outfield in 1985, Herzog had just what he wanted—foul line to foul line speed. "Nobody has ever had a faster or better defensive outfield," he said.

Herzog's Kansas City teams are largely forgotten because they lost the ALCS to the Yankees all three years. But Herzog remembered his 1977 champs as "the best team I've ever managed." The Royals broke up a tight race in late August that year by spinning off 16 wins in a row. They lost a game, then won eight more, winding up with 102 victories.

Herzog took over the Royals in 1975. It was a homecoming for him in two ways. He and his wife lived in Kansas City, and Royals Stadium was, in his words, "a big, Astro-Turf ballpark which was made to order for the way I like to play baseball." The Royals ran, averaging 201 stolen bases a year during their three championship seasons. Shortstop Fred Patek and second baseman Frank White played excellent defense, and so did outfielders Al Cowens and "Famous Amos" Otis. Kansas City had no relief pitcher to match the Yankee bullpen aces of that era, Sparky Lyle and Goose Gossage. But Herzog came up with reasonable facsimiles in right-handers Mark Littell and Doug Bird, and left-handers Steve Mingori and Al Hrabosky.

George Brett isn't particularly fast, but he runs the bases the same way he hits the ball—hard. "If every player approached the game the way George does, it sure would make managing a lot easier," Herzog said. "The toughest thing about managing the Cardinals in the 1985 World Series against the Royals was rooting against George Brett."

Under the tutelage of batting coach Charlie Lau, the Royals learned to hit Herzog-style, slashing liners and hard ground balls through the infield. The team was much like Herzog's Cardinals of later years, with one exception: the Royals had power, and Herzog was glad to use it. George Brett was just coming into his prime, and veteran Hal McRae was the prototype designated hitter. Despite their big ballpark, the 1977 Royals were second in their division in homers with 146, and the power was spread throughout the lineup: 23 homers each for Cowens and John Mayberry, 22 for Brett, 21 for McRae, 17 for Otis, 16 for catcher Darrell Porter. Baseball was blessed with a running-and-slugging team—a mix of styles that won games and excited fans. When he is asked about his preference for the running game, Herzog always replies that he *likes* sluggers. Unlike many other managers, however, Herzog makes speed, defense and relief pitching higher priorities. Make Herzog manager of the Red Sox or Tigers, who play in home run ballparks, and he would look for long-ball hitters. "Geography makes all the difference in baseball these days," Herzog said. True enough, although no one who has watched Herzog's Royals or Cardinals play believes that he could stand to put too many ponderous players in his lineup.

To say that Herzog emphasizes speed, defense and relief pitching is not to hint that he neglects other facets of the game. Successful managers are meticulous. "I've got a file on every hitter I've ever managed against, on every ball he has hit against every pitcher of mine he's ever faced," Herzog wrote in his autobiography. "Baseball is a game of percentages, and I believe in giving myself every percentage advantage."

As a player, Herzog needed advantages. He spent eight seasons in the major leagues as a part-time outfielder. He was fast, and a good defensive

outfielder, but only a fair hitter, posting a .257 lifetime average. With the Orioles in 1961 and 1962, he talked a lot of baseball on the bench with a couple of other part-time players who were learning the trade: Dick Williams, who later won four pennants in a long and nomadic managing career, and Darrell Johnson, who managed eight seasons in the majors, winning a pennant with the Boston Red Sox in 1975.

By then Herzog had already benefited from the teachings of the manager he considers his best tutor: Casey Stengel, who taught the young Herzog at the Yankees' rookie camp in 1955. "He liked to teach baserunning as much as he liked to talk, which was plenty," Herzog said of Stengel. The Yankees farmed Herzog to Denver, where the manager was Ralph Houk—a master, Herzog said, of handling men, as Houk proved in managing the Yankees to three pennants in the early 1960s.

Herzog had excellent tutors. Like Earl Weaver and Casey Stengel, he soaked up the game, never tiring of its details, always looking for an edge, since he was never a good enough player to coast.

Tutoring and an eye for baseball made Herzog one of the most successful, and well-liked, managers in the game. Players throughout the major leagues have said they'd like to play for him. Sportswriters lionize him, and the fans in St. Louis consider him a civic hero. Herzog has come a long way from his first big-league managing job, when he took over a dreadful Texas Rangers club in 1973. At his introductory press conference, Herzog was asked what he thought of his new team. "This is the worst excuse for a big-league club I ever saw," he replied. The Rangers finished last. Whitey Herzog was always a good judge of baseball talent. ◑

On his way to six division titles, three pennants and one world championship in 17 years as a big league manager, Herzog learned the tough lessons that come with his chosen profession. "I thought I did my greatest job of managing in 1979, and yet I got fired," he said. "As a manager, you're always sitting on a keg of dynamite. It's amazing how fast you can get dumb in this game."

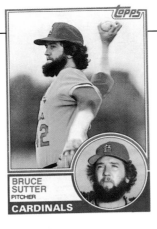

BRUCE
SUTTER
PITCHER

CARDINALS

Bruce Sutter

hen Bruce Sutter's split-finger fastball was humming, it practically took an act of God to put wood on it. "Unhittable," Dick Williams said of Sutter's pitch, which dropped like a rock when it reached the plate. "He's tough," conceded Pete Rose, "just about impossible to hit."

Sutter's unusual delivery elevated him to the top of the heap of relief pitchers: in 1985 he became the first hurler to save more than 20 games in nine consecutive seasons. He holds the National League record for career saves with 300 and is third on the all-time list.

Ironically, it was a bad elbow that lead to Sutter's success. In his first season in the Chicago Cubs' minor league system, he threw a fastball and heard his elbow pop. Surgery repaired the elbow, but he found that he couldn't muster the velocity of his old fastball. "I was struggling," he recalls, "and knew I was through—unless I could come up with a good pitch." That's when Fred Martin, the Cub's roving pitching instructor, introduced Sutter to the forkball.

The forkball has been called a trick pitch, though only its grip is peculiar: the first two fingers are spread into a V with the ball wedged between them. Sutter modified the pitch by gripping the ball not only with his spread fingers, but with his thumb. "I use the thumb all the time for extra velocity and because it makes my ball break that much faster," he said.

Sutter's particular twist made the pitch more fastball than forkball. "I throw it harder than guys who throw forkballs," he said. "My ball has spin and it looks like a fastball, where the forkball is more like a knuckler where there's not much spin to it."

The split-finger fastball proved difficult for Sutter to master. "It took me three years to learn how to throw it, how to control it. It was awkward at the start," he recalls. "I'd try to use it in a game and it seemed like I was always bouncing it in the dirt."

By 1977, his sophomore major league season, he had mastered it well enough to save 31 games for the Cubs with a 1.35 ERA. "Playing behind him in my first two years with the Cubs," said outfielder Bill Buckner, "he was the biggest mismatch against the hitter I have ever seen. He made good hitters miss by two feet." Sutter's pitch broke so sharply at the plate that some compared it to a baseball rolling off a table.

Just two years later he became the third reliever in history to win the coveted Cy Young Award. Even though the Cubs finished next to last in their division with 80 wins and 82 losses, Sutter saved 37 games, equaling the all-time NL record.

In 1981 Sutter was traded to the Cardinals and manager Whitey Herzog, who prized relief pitching perhaps above all else. Sutter's arm proved to be just what Herzog needed in 1982, though an early-season slump caused the manager to lament, "If he doesn't do it, we ain't gonna have a very good season. He's the key to the whole thing."

Sutter didn't let Herzog—or the team—down. In 70 games he led the league with 36 saves, an effort that helped the Cards win the NL pennant. His play in the World Series was no less spectacular: he won one game and saved two others, including Game 7, as St. Louis beat the Milwaukee Brewers.

By the end of his career, in 1988, Sutter had pitched in 661 games without ever starting. When asked about this he said, "I think I'd be nervous as a starting pitcher. Now, I'm completely relaxed for the first five innings of a game. As a relief pitcher, you never have time to get nervous, but you never get the ideal situation either. It's feast or famine." For much of Sutter's career, it was a feast.

Bruce Sutter's split-finger fastball broke so sharply that even though it usually wound up below the knees, even good hitters couldn't lay off it. "The best way to hit against Sutter is to go up there without a bat," said Pete Rose. "You'd probably walk."

BRUCE SUTTER

Right-Handed Pitcher
Chicago Cubs 1976-1980
St. Louis Cardinals 1981-1984
Atlanta Braves 1985-1986, 1988

GAMES	**661**
INNINGS	
Career	**1,040⅔**
Season High	**122⅔**
WINS	
Career	**68**
Season High	**9**
LOSSES	
Career	**71**
Season High	**10**
WINNING PERCENTAGE	
Career	**.489**
Season High	**.700**
ERA	
Career	**2.84**
Season Low	**1.35**
SAVES	
Career *(3rd all time)*	**300**
Season High *(4th all time)*	**45**
STRIKEOUTS	
Career	**861**
Season High	**129**
WALKS	
Career	**309**
Season High	**34**
WORLD SERIES	**1982**
CY YOUNG AWARD	**1979**

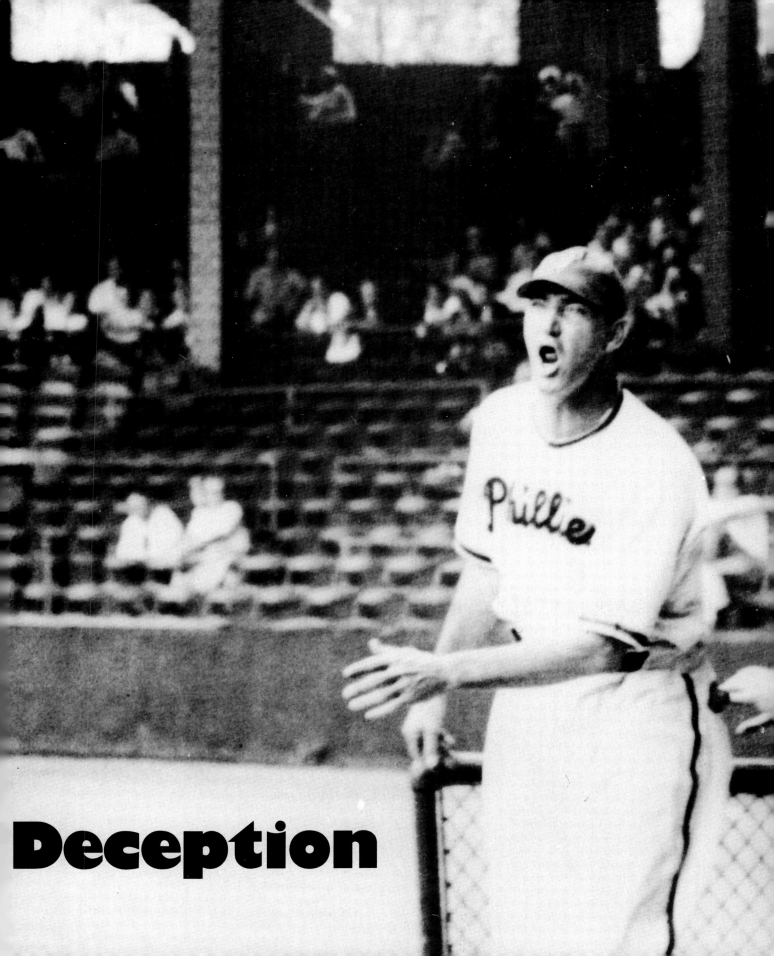

Deception

The Giants' Willie Mays was fast—and smart. Mays wore caps that were too big so they would fly off his head as he was running the bases or chasing a fly ball, thereby making him seem even faster than he really was.

All's fair in love and baseball. Players that have to wander near the opposing dugout—like Giants catcher Walker Cooper (preceding page)—are especially inviting targets for abuse. As Cooper went after a foul pop, Phillies pitcher Schoolboy Rowe tried to break his concentration. It didn't work.

hird game of the 1972 World Series, eighth inning. With Cincinnati leading Oakland, 1–0, and one out in the Cincinnati eighth, Johnny Bench came to bat with Joe Morgan on third base and Bobby Tolan on first. Rollie Fingers, the Athletics' ace reliever, worked the count on Bench to 3 and 2, but as he did so, Tolan stole second. That took away the double-play opportunity. The situation was obvious: the A's now would walk Bench. After all, he was a dangerous hitter and he led the National League that season in homers, with 40, and in RBI, with 125. But he wasn't fast. A walk would fill the bases, restoring the double-play opportunity.

Dick Williams, the Oakland manager, and Gene Tenace, the catcher, conferred with Fingers on the mound. Williams pointed to first base and returned to the dugout. Tenace stood and held his glove to the right, the classic signal for a ball. Bench let the bat rest on his shoulder. Fingers stretched —and fired strike three down the middle, Tenace crouching to catch it.

The A's still lost the game, 1–0, but they had managed to fool Johnny Bench. A play that deceptive can't be used often, but if saved for just the right spot, as it was in this case, it can work even against the best.

Deception is the hidden weapon in a manager's arsenal, the final wrinkle in a pitcher's repertoire, the last straw in defeat. In football, the quarterback tries to deceive the defense on virtually every play, faking handoffs or sending receivers on pass patterns designed only to draw defensive players out of position. Fakery is less prevalent in baseball. It requires inventive thinking, superb playacting and the patience to save a pet play for that one situation where it might win a game. Use it more often and the opposition will look for it, killing the play and wasting the work that went into perfecting it.

If the players don't pull it off right or the opposing players are alert enough to intervene, the work might well be wasted. But a successful manager—and successful players—will work on those rare gems of deception anyway, knowing that if a trick play wins one or two games a year, it can make the difference between first and second place.

The Baltimore Orioles finished first in 1979, and manager Earl Weaver nailed down one of their victories with a play the Orioles had practiced over and over during spring training and saved for the right moment. The scenario required a tie game in the ninth or an extra inning—a situation in which one run would win the game. Oriole runners had to be on first and third with two out, the opposing pitcher should be left-handed and if he was inexperienced, so much the better.

It might sound like a long shot, but Weaver's moment came against the Chicago White Sox. Two were out in the bottom of the 12th; Oriole Eddie Murray was on third base, Doug DeCinces was on first and Guy Hoffman, a rookie southpaw, was pitching for Chicago. The Baltimore crowd was on its feet, yelling for a hit.

Hoffman stretched—and to his surprise saw DeCinces break for second and lose his footing. With the easy pickoff at hand, Hoffman stepped toward first. His teammates were shouting something—it was hard to hear, because the crowd was in an uproar—and Hoffman turned around, just in time to see Murray cross the plate with the winning run. Weaver's play called for Murray to break for home just as DeCinces faked his pratfall at first.

Roberto Clemente, the Pirates' great right fielder from 1955 through 1972, practiced a different kind of playacting. On a hit to right, Clemente bobbled the ball, luring the batter into trying for second base. Clemente's

Catcher Gary Carter helps his team win with his bat, his glove, his arm . . . and his mouth. His favorite method of distracting hitters is to make them laugh with a pitch on the way. "I'll do anything so their mind isn't a hundred percent on hitting or the pitch," he said.

In the Pinch

It's the toughest job in baseball: coming in cold off the bench with the game on the line, facing a 95-mph fastball from the likes of Goose Gossage, or Gregg Olson's knee-buckling curve. But a few players thrive in the pressure-packed role of pinch-hitter. Tommy Davis hit .320 as a pinch-hitter. Cliff Johnson hit 20 homers as a pinch-hitter for a 7.2 home run percentage, a mark that—had he maintained it throughout his career—would rank second behind Babe Ruth on the all-time list. Below are the leaders among pinch-hitters in career batting average, hits and home runs.

BATTING AVERAGE

NAME	AVERAGE	YEARS
Tommy Davis	.320	1959-1977
Frenchy Bordagaray	.312	1934-1945
Frankie Baumholtz	.307	1947-1957
Red Schoendienst	.303	1945-1963
Bob Fothergill	.300	1922-1933
Dave Philley	.299	1941-1962
Manny Mota	.297	1962-1982
Ted Easterly	.296	1909-1915
Rance Mulliniks	.296	1977-
Harvey Hendrick	.295	1923-1934
Larry Herndon	.294	1974-1988
Manny Sanguillen	.288	1967-1980
Thad Bosley	.286	1977-
Smoky Burgess	.286	1949-1967
Rick Miller	.286	1971-1985

PINCH HITS

NAME	HITS	YEARS
Manny Mota	150	1962-1982
Smoky Burgess	145	1949-1967
Greg Gross	143	1973-1989
Jose Morales	123	1973-1984
Jerry Lynch	116	1954-1966
Red Lucas	114	1923-1938
Steve Braun	113	1971-1985
Terry Crowley	108	1969-1983
Gates Brown	107	1963-1975
Mike Lum	103	1967-1981
Rusty Staub	100	1963-1985
Jim Dwyer	96	1973-1989
Larry Biittner	95	1970-1983
Vic Davalillo	95	1963-1980
Jerry Hairston	94	1973-1989

HOME RUNS

NAME	HRs	YEARS
Cliff Johnson	20	1972-1986
Jerry Lynch	18	1954-1966
Gates Brown	16	1963-1975
Smoky Burgess	16	1949-1967
Willie McCovey	16	1959-1980
George Crowe	14	1952-1961
Joe Adcock	12	1950-1966
Bob Cerv	12	1951-1962
Jose Morales	12	1973-1984
Graig Nettles	12	1967-1988
Jeff Burroughs	11	1970-1985
Jay Johnstone	11	1966-1985
Fred Whitfield	11	1962-1970
Cy Williams	11	1912-1930

Statistics are complete through the 1989 season.

bobble was a fake, and his arm was the best in baseball: out at second. Willie Mays of the Giants worked that play in reverse. In an All-Star game, Rocky Colavito was playing left field. Mays knew that Colavito liked to show off his powerful throwing arm, so when Mays doubled to left, he rounded second and hesitated, appearing to lean back toward second. Colavito threw to second, and by the time he was committed, Mays was on his way to third.

Ty Cobb, the ultimate baserunning strategist, invented a play that worked when the Tigers had runners on second and third. The runner on second would take a good lead on each pitch and take his time returning to the bag. Unsuspecting catchers viewed this as a pickoff opportunity. But as soon as the catcher threw toward second, both runners took off, the lead runner scoring and the other advancing to third.

In an attempt to fool runners, infielders often pantomime, setting themselves as if to catch a grounder when the ball actually has been driven into the outfield. It rarely works, but Maury Wills, the Dodgers' shortstop of the 1960s, embarrassed a young Montreal baserunner on a long drive that hit the fence in left center. Realizing that the youngster on first had lost sight of the ball, Wills looked up as if for a pop fly, calling "I got it! I got it!" The runner reversed course and headed back to first, passing the batter, who was en route to second. The batter was out for passing another baserunner, and the throw from the outfield beat the kid back to first base: double play.

Some tricks call for offstage help. In a college game, Florida Technological University pulled a teamwork pantomime play employing the catcher, the shortstop and a player on the bench. A fast University of Miami runner was on first base, and the situation called for a steal. The runner broke. As he did, a

Intimidation was Yankee reliever Ryne Duren's favorite play, and he'd get the job done before the batter even stepped into the box. Duren, a wild fastballer in the 1950s and 1960s with 20/200 vision, would purposely throw a warmup pitch yards over the catcher's head, making hitters think twice about digging in at the plate.

Tech player in the dugout whacked two bats together, producing a sound like a batted ball. The catcher caught the pitch and threw a pop-up toward the shortstop, who yelled, "I got it! I got it!" The runner had stolen second, but he had heard the ball "hit," and now he saw the shortstop camped under a pop fly. So he headed hopelessly back to first and was thrown out.

When he was managing the Brooklyn Dodgers in 1934, Casey Stengel invented a great play that also involved acting skills. With a runner on third and three balls on the batter, Stengel's pitcher would fire a beanball—the last pitch anyone could *imagine* in such a situation. As he released the ball, the pitcher would shout, "Look out!" as if the pitch had slipped. The batter would fall out of the way, the runner on third, taking a lead, would freeze in fear and surprise, and Stengel's catcher—knowing the play was on—would stand, grab the inside pitch and fire it to third base, picking off the thoroughly muddled runner.

Trouble was, Stengel's players were a muddled bunch, and the throw usually went into left field, either because the catcher threw wild, the third baseman missed the sign and failed to cover, or both. Stengel abandoned the play, but Gabby Hartnett, the Cubs' great catcher, used it successfully in Game 3 of the 1935 World Series. With one out in the Detroit sixth, Goose Goslin singled and Pete Fox tripled him home. With Billy Rogell at bat, Hartnett called the "beanball play" and picked Fox off third. This time, Hartnett didn't wait for a three-ball count against the batter. So Rogell was still up—and he took a called third strike to end the inning. The Cubs went on to lose the Series, but they won Game 3, 3–2.

A similarly deceptive play helped the Cubs win a late-season game over Pittsburgh and gave them the edge they needed to win a tight pennant race.

Continued on page 152

Luis Tiant's baffling array of twists, dips, flutters and release points drove batters batty in the 1960s and 1970s. "Luis Tiant comes from everywhere except between his legs," said broadcaster Curt Gowdy. In 1968 Tiant held opposing hitters to a .168 batting average—the lowest in history.

CHANCE, CHICAGO NAT'L

Frank Chance

He was part of baseball's best-known double-play combination, the one that inspired the most enduring of baseball ditties: "Tinker to Evers to Chance." In fact, Chicago shortstop Joe Tinker, second baseman Johnny Evers and first baseman Frank Chance turned few double plays by modern standards. But they excelled defensively, handling bunts and other plays with a prescience that reflected the skill and guidance of their manager: first baseman Chance, who was dubbed "the Peerless Leader" when he led the Cubs to pennants in 1906, 1907, 1908 and 1910.

Chance broke into the majors as a catcher in 1898. He wasn't very good at the position, and he resisted when manager Frank Selee asked him to play first base in 1902. Chance finally made the switch and quickly became one of the National League's best first basemen. He also excelled at bat and on the bases, hitting over .300 four times and twice leading the league in stolen bases.

Chance replaced Selee as Cub manager in midseason 1905. John McGraw's New York Giants dominated the NL back then, but McGraw encountered a worthy rival in Chance, whose Cubs romped to runaway pennants in 1906 and 1907. Chicago enjoyed its only streetcar Series in 1906, when the Cubs were favored to beat the White Sox, who had hit only seven home runs all season and batted .230 as a team. But "the Hitless Wonders," as the Sox were called, upset Chance's club four games to two. In 1907 the Cubs won their first World Series, beating the Tigers—and Ty Cobb—four games to none, with one tie.

The 1908 NL race may be the most famous in history. The Cubs edged the Giants by one game af-

ter an apparent Giant victory was nullified by "Merkle's boner"—actually, a shrewd play by Evers, the Chicago second baseman, who called for the ball and tagged second base, forcing out Fred Merkle of the Giants, who had trotted to the dugout rather than bother to touch second on a ninth-inning hit that appeared to decide the game.

Cobb batted .368 for Detroit in the 1908 World Series, but Chance outhit him at .421 while managing the Cubs to their second straight world championship. After a second-place finish in 1909, the Cubs won again in 1910; McGraw's Giants finished second, 13 games behind. Chance had established himself as one of baseball's first dynasty managers, winning four pennants in five years. He encountered another dynasty manager in the 1910 World Series: Connie Mack, whose Philadelphia Athletics won the Series four games to one. Still, Chance again acquitted himself proudly, batting .353 and leading the Cubs in RBI with four.

When the Cubs sagged to second place in 1911 and third in 1912, Chance was fired. His playing career was all but over, hastened by a number of beanings, including one that required surgery to relieve blood clots. He got two more managing opportunities, but with bad teams. His New York Yankees finished seventh in 1913 and again in 1914, and his Boston Red Sox came in last in 1923.

In 1924 Chance was due for a return to Chicago, as manager of the White Sox. But poor health forced him to stay home, and he died that September. In 1946 he was elected to the Baseball Hall of Fame with his shortstop, Joe Tinker, to join second baseman Johnny Evers, who had been inducted in 1939.

FRANK CHANCE

Manager
Chicago Cubs 1905-1912
New York Yankees 1913-1914
Boston Red Sox 1923
Hall of Fame 1946

GAMES	**1,622**
WINS	
Career	**946**
Season High *(1st all time)*	**116**
LOSSES	
Career	**648**
Season High	**94**
WINNING PERCENTAGE	
Career *(6th all time)*	**.593**
Season High *(1st all time)*	**.763**
PENNANTS	**1906, 1907,**
	1908, 1910
WORLD CHAMPIONSHIPS	**1907,**
	1908

Respected as a player and manager, Frank Chance was a fierce competitor and a rigid taskmaster. He forbade his players from shaking hands with the opposition while in uniform. "You're a ballplayer and not a society dancer at a pink tea," he said. "I want to see some fight in you."

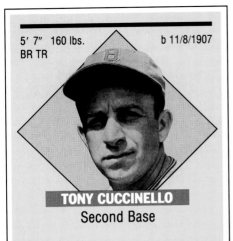

5' 7" 160 lbs.
BR TR

b 11/8/1907

TONY CUCCINELLO
Second Base

Most ballplayers can accept spikings and brushbacks as part of the game. But the hidden ball trick—that's humiliation. And many a player must have wished a painful and untimely demise for second baseman Tony Cuccinello, a master of the stunt.

Cuccinello came up to the majors with Cincinnati in 1930. He moved to the Dodgers in 1936 and then closed out his career with the Chicago White Sox from 1943 to 1945. He was a solid fielder who led the NL in double plays four times, assists twice, and putouts once even with stiff fielding competition from the likes of Cub second baseman Billy Herman. Cuccinello hit over .300 five times, and in 1945, at 37, was almost the oldest man ever to win a batting championship. On the final day of the season, Snuffy Stirnweiss, credited with a hit on a play that most observers said was an error, passed Cuccinello, .309 to .308.

But Cuccinello's forte was the hidden ball trick, and he turned several pros into pawns. One of his victims was Ernie Lombardi. "You tag me," warned the 230-pound catcher when Cuccinello showed him the ball, "and I'll punch you right in the nose." Cuccinello let him walk off the field untagged. But during a game the day after Cleveland player-manager Lou Boudreau told the press the hidden ball trick was obsolete, Boudreau found himself on base —only until Cuccinello suddenly produced a ball and tagged him out.

Giants manager Leo Durocher was a professional agitator. He annoyed umpires, opponents, even his own players, but he was one of the great bench jockeys of all time. "Stick it in his ear!" was one of Durocher's favorite lines to disturb opposing hitters.

The Cubs led Pittsburgh by one run. With one out in the Pirate eighth, the Chicago pitcher walked two batters in a row. Ed Reulbach was called in to relieve, walked the next batter on four pitches and threw two balls to the following batter. Reulbach was steaming—the bases were loaded. He yelled at the umpire, pitched, and when the ump called ball three, Reulbach angrily took the catcher's return throw and hurled it toward the dugout! The Pirate runners took off—but were caught short. The Cubs had a play on: a once-in-a-lifetime play. Del Howard, the Cubs' first baseman, had slipped down the first-base line between Reulbach and the dugout. He took Reulbach's throw and fired to catcher Johnny Kling, who tagged the runner sliding home and threw to Harry Steinfeldt at third base to nab the runner coming in there. The Cubs held their one-run lead, winning the crucial game.

A similar but even better play—the "phantom pickoff"—was pulled off in a recent College World Series. With a runner on first, the pitcher stepped off the mound and threw wildly—or so it seemed—to the first baseman, who dived futilely for the ball. The defensive team's bullpen was in line with the mound and first; the bullpen players scattered. Even the first-base umpire ran down the line, looking for the ball. The runner took off for second and was thrown out easily by the pitcher, who had kept the ball all the while.

Bullpen benchwarmers stretched a double into a homer for the Chicago Cubs on July 1, 1958. Chicago's Tony Taylor hit a rope over third base. The ball landed fair, then bounded foul toward the Cub bullpen, with the Giants' left fielder, Leon Wagner, in pursuit. The Cubs jumped up and looked under the bench, so Wagner did, too; he had lost sight of the ball. In fact, the ball was resting 20 feet past the bullpen. Taylor got an inside-the-park homer.

In addition to being one of the finest fielding shortops of the 1930s and 1940s, the Yankees' Frankie Crosetti (above, sliding) was a master at stealing signs and the hidden-ball trick.

ntimidation is a useful weapon. The Yankees of Babe Ruth and Lou Gehrig used to intimidate World Series opponents by repeatedly smashing balls over the fence during batting practice. There was nothing deceptive about that Yankee power, but before the 1978 All-Star Game, Pete Rose borrowed the ploy and added a deceptive twist. He obtained a batch of extra-lively Japanese baseballs for use in batting practice by the National League All-Stars. What a show! The NL hitters looked like supermen, and Rose's psych job may have contributed to the NL's 7–3 win.

The American League prepared to add two teams in 1961, and it allowed the new franchises to draft a number of unprotected players from the established teams. Paul Richards, manager of the Orioles, wondered how he could keep the expansion teams from drafting a prized Oriole rookie, Chuck Hinton. Inspiration struck: Richards ordered Hinton to run into the outfield wall in pursuit of a fungo and feign serious injury. Hinton did his best, but the expansion Washington Senators drafted him anyway, and he played in their outfield for four seasons.

When you're trying to deceive someone, a little stupidity on the other side helps. In a game between the Dodgers and the Giants in 1916, Brooklyn's Ollie O'Mara was sent up to bunt; Hy Myers was on first base and Jack Coombs was on second. O'Mara dropped a short bunt down the third-base line and lumbered toward first. Catcher Bill Rariden thought he had a chance to get the lead runner, so he threw to third—wildly. Rariden, anxious to keep his error from allowing a run or two, yelled "Foul ball!" in hopes umpire Bill Klem would call it foul.

Klem wasn't fooled, but O'Mara was. He turned around and walked back toward the plate. Klem yelled "Fair ball!" O'Mara, however, would

One reason they call it the "home field advantage" is because it's fairly easy to manipulate the field to the home team's advantage. When the Pirates obtained right-handed slugger Hank Greenberg in 1947, they built a fence that shortened left field by 30 feet. It was christened "Greenberg Gardens," but became more famous as "Kiner's Korner," when slugger Ralph Kiner used it to win seven straight home run titles from 1946 to 1952.

have none of it. He hadn't seen the wild throw, hadn't sorted out who was yelling what and cast his own vote. "Foul ball!" O'Mara yelled. "Fair ball!" Klem yelled again.

Rariden's wild throw rolled to the fence. Coombs and Myers scored; at least O'Mara had carried out his instructions to sacrifice. Four Dodger teammates tried to hustle him to first base, but he resisted, still set on the idea that his bunt had rolled foul. He was thrown out at first, from deep left field.

The hidden ball trick is *old.* In 1911 *Baseball Magazine* had this to say about it: "This is one of the oldest tricks known to the fan. In fact it is so old that every time it is used successfully the player who is put out as a result of it is hooted by the spectators." Rabbit Maranville, a colorful shortstop who earned a niche in the Hall of Fame during a 23-year career that ended in 1935, starred in two hidden-ball incidents. Hy Myers of the Dodgers took a lead off second base, and Maranville stepped between Myers and the bag. "Why, Hy, what are you doing standing clear out here?" Maranville asked. Myers sarcastically asked where he should stand. "What," replied Maranville, "and with me holding the ball?" He tagged Myers out.

Twenty years into his career, Maranville himself was victimized by the hidden-ball trick. He was embarrassed, and the manager of the team's hotel invited him to a feast, telling Maranville it would make him feel better. The meal concluded with Maranville's favorite dessert: a heaping dish of chocolate ice cream. Maranville dug in. His spoon struck something hard. It was a hidden baseball.

On August 31, 1987, a minor league catcher named Dave Bresnahan gave the old hidden-ball trick a twist that entertained fans throughout the country. Bresnahan was catching for Williamsport, Pennsylvania. The Phillies of Reading, Pennsylvania, had the winning run on third with two outs in the ninth. Bresnahan made up an excuse to go to the dugout and came back with a raw, peeled potato hidden in his glove. He caught the next pitch and, as if trying to pick the runner off third, threw the potato into left field. The runner ran home, where Bresnahan was waiting with the ball. Alas, officials on the scene took a stern view. The runner was ruled safe. Bresnahan was fined $50 and released; he was hitting only .149 anyway. But the trick was so funny —so against the grain—that Bresnahan became something of a celebrity: he was given a special day by the Williamsport team a year later, and his number was painted on the outfield fence. As Dick Williams and Earl Weaver might have said, not every trick works, but it's worth trying. ◑

Catcher Tony Pena (above, with St. Louis) has one of the game's more unusual squats, but he's even more creative in his efforts to distract hitters. His favorite trick is to spit on the batter's shoes as the pitcher is releasing the ball.

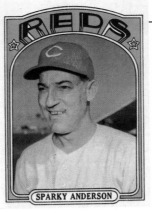

SPARKY ANDERSON

Sparky Anderson

There are those who feel that managing a major league baseball team is a science, a discipline requiring a deep understanding of the laws of probability, the nuances of strategy and the complexities of human psychology.

George "Sparky" Anderson is not among them.

"There ain't no genius who ever managed in this game," he once said. "I ain't no genius. No one is. Just because you're a manager doesn't make you no smarter than the next guy."

His modesty and grammar notwithstanding, Anderson is one shrewd baseball man. In his first 18 years as a major league manager, his teams won five pennants and three World Series. He also became the first manager to lead clubs in both leagues to more than 100 victories in a season and the only manager to win a world championship in each league.

No one would have dared to predict that kind of success in 1970 when Anderson, in an announcement that stunned all of southwestern Ohio and puzzled baseball fans everywhere, was named the manager of the Cincinnati Reds. Not only was he a mere 35 at the time, but he also had all of one year of major league coaching experience, and that as a third-base coach for the fledgling San Diego Padres. On top of that, Anderson, despite a feisty personality that earned him his nickname, had played only one year in the majors. In 1959 he had been a classic good-field, no-hit second baseman for the Philadelphia Phillies, and his .218 batting average that season got him shipped back to the minors for good.

His demotion to the AAA club in Toronto was the beginning of the end of his playing career. But it also was the point at which he began preparing for his true life's work. Anderson watched closely as Charlie Dressen ran the team, looking for constants in his thinking, absorbing rivulets of strategy: how Dressen never hesitated to yank a starter whose pitches began coming higher and higher through the strike zone, how he let a starting pitcher work out of two jams but never a third, and how he forced the opposing manager to use up his bench and bullpen.

With his newfound dugout wisdom and a head of prematurely white hair, Sparky got his own team in 1964. He led Class AAA Toronto to a respectable 80–72 record. At first, Anderson managed by tantrum, screaming at players and umpires alike. Then, as he learned to become more patient, he became a winner. Over the next four years he moved up the minor league ladder, and each time he took over a team, it got better. In 1968 his Asheville team won the Southern League pennant and major league executives took notice.

Anderson leaped to the Padres a year later, and in 1970 a surprise call came from Cincinnati general manager Bob Howsam: was he interested in managing the Reds? Sparky jumped at the chance but knew he was heading into stormy seas. The man he replaced, Dave Bristol, had been very popular with his players, but he was dumped because he hadn't been able to deliver a champion. That first year the Reds went to the World Series. They lost to Baltimore, but the intimidating identity of the Big Red Machine, with Anderson at the helm, had been established.

As the team became a National League powerhouse, Sparky's odd and unorthodox style became one of its trademarks. More than most managers, he operated by instinct, sometimes ignoring the per-

Sparky Anderson never considered himself a brilliant manager, but he managed to keep a bunch of high profile stars like Reds shortstop Davey Concepcion (right) happy and productive. "What Sparky Anderson does best," said second baseman Joe Morgan, "is keep us aiming toward one thing, winning."

dency to yank pitchers at the first sign of trouble earned him the nickname "Captain Hook," but it also kept the Reds in games. During one stretch in Cincinnati's 1975 championship season, the Reds' pitching staff went a record 45 straight games without a complete game. The team won 32 of them. Anderson showed that a starter needed only to give the team six strong innings to get his job done, a notion that's now accepted wisdom.

The Reds rolled to championships in 1975 and 1976, but when Sparky couldn't deliver a third, they let him go. He wasn't out of baseball for long, though. Partway through the 1979 season, the Detroit Tigers hired him, hoping he could repeat his magic in the American League. Anderson, ever the optimist, predicted a championship by the time his five-year contract ran out. Baseball experts scoffed. In Detroit, Anderson had talented young players like Alan Trammell, Lou Whitaker, Kirk Gibson and Lance Parrish, but nothing to match the Cincinnati superstars he had managed.

The team steadily improved, but through 1983, the best Detroit managed was a second-place finish in the AL East. Skeptics began to suggest that the game had passed Sparky by, that his rah-rah tactics didn't work on millionaire players. What the Tigers needed, they argued, were deep-thinking managers who relied on stratagems, not motivation, to win games.

But in 1984 the Tigers got off to the fastest start in major league history, winning 35 of their first 40 games. They coasted to an AL East championship with 104 wins, finishing 15 games ahead of second-place Toronto. In the playoffs, the Tigers made quick work of the Kansas City Royals, then destroyed the San Diego Padres in the World Series. In postseason play Detroit lost only one game.

The Tiger players were quick to credit Anderson for his patience and his unending support. "People have been hard on me here," said Kirk Gibson, "and Sparky knows how to handle that a lot better than I do, so he stayed behind me." Teammate Parrish added, "The best thing about him is his desire to communicate with the rest of the club. He's gotten me to be the best I can in every aspect of my game."

Anderson showed that he belonged on any list of the best major league managers. And he had done it his way. "My secret," Sparky said simply, "was to tell players to go out and make me smart."

centages that others religiously followed. He might intentionally walk the same batter three times in a game or let a left-handed pitcher stay in to face a right-handed batter. He relied more on his memory than on detailed notes to determine how a particular hitter or pitcher should be handled. More motivator than tactician, Anderson focused on players' mental attitudes more than their batting averages.

"Ninety per cent of managing is psychology and how you keep your players prepared to play," said Joe Morgan, one of Anderson's stars. "When I played for Sparky, the attitude he had for us was the reason we won all those championships. I really didn't think of him as my manager, but more like he was part of my family—and I'll do a lot more for my family than I will for my manager."

Even those players who had every reason to feel disgruntled, such as the Reds' starting pitchers, saw that Anderson's methods got results. His ten-

SPARKY ANDERSON

Manager
Cincinnati Reds 1970-1978
Detroit Tigers 1979-

GAMES *(10th all time)*	**3,285**
WINS	
Career *(10th all time)*	**1,837**
Season High *(7th all time)*	**108**
LOSSES	
Career	**1,446**
Season High	**103**
WINNING PERCENTAGE	
Career	**.560**
Season High	**.667**
DIVISION TITLES	**1970, 1972,**
1973, 1975, 1976, 1984, 1987	
PENNANTS	**1970, 1972, 1975,**
	1976, 1984
WORLD CHAMPIONSHIPS	**1975,**
	1976, 1984

Anderson's reputation as the quickest hook in the majors followed him from Cincinnati (left, with Johnny Bench) to Detroit (opposite). In 1984, his Tigers won 105 games in the regular season and went on to win a world championship, yet the Detroit pitching staff finished with just 19 complete games, 10th highest in the American League.

OAKS WIN FIRST FLAG IN 21 YEARS

P.C.L Champs

Casey
at the Helm

asey Stengel didn't invent platooning, but he raised it to a fine art. Stengel managed the New York Yankees for 12 seasons, from 1949 through 1960. He shuffled players in and out of the lineup as they had never been shuffled before, and although his players complained when they were benched, they had little to complain about at World Series time. Stengel's Yankees won ten pennants and seven world championships, and he was forever immortalized as the master of platoon baseball.

Even the term *platooning* was first used to describe Stengel's lineup strategy. The term was borrowed from football, which was then in transition from the old system, under which substitution was limited and most players played both offense and defense, to the modern system of separate offensive and defensive teams. Sportswriters called this "two-platoon football," and in May 1949 Harold Rosenthal of the *New York Herald-Tribune* wrote that Stengel was "two-platooning" his outfielders.

In fact, Stengel was platooning at three positions. Against left-handed pitchers, he usually played Billy Johnson at third base, and Hank Bauer and Johnny Lindell in the outfield; all three batted right. Against right-handed pitchers, Stengel played Bobby Brown at third base, and Gene Woodling and Cliff Mapes in the outfield. Brown, Woodling and Mapes batted left-handed.

Of course, most right-handed batters hit better against lefties than against right-handed pitchers. Curveballs and sliders are easier to

*Casey Stengel managed baseball's greatest team—the Yankees—and its worst—the Mets. He remains the game's most beloved philosopher. The secret to managing, he said, "is to keep the five guys who hate you away from the five guys who are **undecided.**"*

In 1949 Stengel's best move was putting Joe DiMaggio back in the lineup on June 28, the instant his injured heel healed. Making his season debut against the Red Sox in Fenway Park, DiMaggio hit four homers and drove in nine runs in a three-game sweep. DiMaggio hit .346 the rest of the way, and the Yanks wound up beating Boston in a one-game playoff for the pennant.

Stengel's playing career mirrored his managing career—the better the team, the better he did. He was traded to the New York Giants in 1922, and proceeded to have his two finest seasons—hitting .368 and .339, respectively, as the Giants were NL champions in 1922 and 1923.

hit. To a right-handed batter, a good curve or slider thrown by a right-handed pitcher looks inside—sometimes frighteningly inside—and the batter might lean back just as the pitch breaks over the plate for a strike. But if the pitcher is left-handed, his curve or slider breaks *toward* the batter, it's easier to watch all the way and it never looks as if it might hit him. For a left-handed batter, the reverse is true: a righty is easier to hit. It all comes down to seeing the ball better when it comes from the opposite side—a major reason for platooning.

In 1949 Stengel was building a third Yankee dynasty, and his methods struck some traditionalists as heretical. Miller Huggins, manager of the great Yankee teams of the 1920s, didn't platoon much. Neither did Joe McCarthy, whose Yankee powerhouses won four straight world championships from 1936 through 1939.

Even though Stengel didn't have as good a team, his record surpassed those of Huggins and McCarthy: Stengel's Yanks won five straight world championships. His team is remembered for the explosive hitting of Mickey Mantle and Yogi Berra, the superb play of shortstop Phil Rizzuto, and the pitching of Whitey Ford, Vic Raschi, Eddie Lopat and Allie Reynolds. But those stars couldn't play every position, and Stengel's platooning made the most of his other players—players who were good but not great, and whose talents were magnified by judicious use of the right man against the right pitcher—or, we should say, against the *left* pitcher.

Not that Stengel platooned automatically; in the outfield, he didn't intend to platoon at all. He went into spring training of 1949, his first year as Yankee manager, with a veteran all-star outfield: Tommy Henrich, Charlie

Keller and the great Joe DiMaggio. But Keller and DiMaggio suffered injuries, and Stengel's platooning made the best of the situation.

Believe it or not, Stengel's Yankees were underdogs even before injuries felled Keller and DiMaggio. In the 1949 preseason poll of baseball writers, 119 picked the Boston Red Sox to win the American League pennant. The Cleveland Indians, who had beaten the Red Sox in a one-game playoff to capture the 1948 pennant, were favored by 79 writers, the Yankees by only 6. And things got worse during spring training: Keller tore muscles in his side, and DiMaggio underwent surgery after suffering a recurrence of an inflamed right heel caused by a bone spur. Arthur Daley, sports columnist for *The New York Times,* viewed the Yankees without DiMaggio as forlorn: "Stengel never had a first-division team," Daley wrote. "It could very well be that his record in that respect will remain unbroken."

Daley was right about Stengel's record. In the 1930s and early 1940s Stengel managed the Brooklyn Dodgers for three seasons and the Boston Braves for six. His teams finished in the second division every year. Just before the 1943 season, Stengel was hit by a car as he walked across a street in Boston. He suffered a broken leg and missed part of the season. The Braves finished sixth, and Dave Egan, a Boston sportswriter, wrote: "The man who did the most for baseball in Boston in 1943 was the motorist who ran Stengel down two days before the opening game and kept him away from the Braves for two months."

The young Yankees of 1949 may have looked weak to writers spoiled by past Yankee greatness, but they looked good to Stengel. "I never had so many good players before," he said. "I'm with a lot of real pros. When I think of some of those other teams I had, I was wondering whether I

Outfielder Gene Woodling didn't like being platooned, and he wasn't shy about letting Stengel know how he felt. The two locked horns numerous times, but when Stengel took over the Mets in 1962, Woodling was the only one of his ex-Yankee players that Stengel obtained.

Yogi Berra (forcing out Baltimore's Billy Hunter) gained most of his fame with his bat and his mouth, but he was an outstanding defensive catcher and handler of pitchers. He once played 148 consecutive games without an error, and Ted Williams, who was hardly known for passing out idle compliments, said Berra "knew the little things that make the pitcher great."

was managing a baseball team or a golf course. You know what I mean—one pro to a club."

Stengel worked hard—and worked his players hard—to fit the pieces together. Yogi Berra, 23, had proved himself a promising hitter with power, but his teammates joked about his inept catching. Stengel asked Bill Dickey, a great Yankee catcher of the previous era, to work with Berra, and to everyone's surprise the young catcher applied himself and began to improve. "Bill is learning me all his experiences," said Berra. "You can observe a lot by watching." Those were among the first of the spontaneous Yogi-isms that endeared Berra to a generation of fans.

The Yankee veterans, though, were perplexed by Stengel's spring training regimen. He would play a man at one position on Wednesday, another on Thursday and a third on Friday. He held DiMaggio in awe but was brusque with other players, calling them by their numbers instead of their names—Stengel always had trouble remembering names.

But Stengel knew the score—maybe more so than anyone else in baseball. He was bright, and he had been in baseball virtually forever—to be precise, since 1910, when Stengel, 19, joined the minor league Kansas City Blues as a pitcher. He pitched badly but hit well, was converted to the outfield and began absorbing lessons that he later passed on to the young Yankees. Stengel's manager, Danny Shay, drilled him on playing rebounds off the outfield wall, a skill Stengel was slow to acquire. "Play the angles! Play the angles!" shouted Shay. Stengel replied, "If you want somebody to play the angles, why don't you hire a pool player?" The manager, as usual, had the last word. "You ought to be a pool player," he yelled to Stengel. "You've got a head as hard as a billiard ball."

Playing for Montgomery, Alabama, in 1912, Stengel struck up a friendship with Norm Elberfeld, a legendary shortstop who had played 13 seasons in the major leagues and had managed the Yankees in 1908, when they were called the New York Highlanders. Elberfeld was a little pepperpot, a scrapper of the Billy Martin or Pete Rose variety. They called him "the Tabasco Kid" and "Kid Elberfeld." By 1912 he was near the end of his career, playing shortstop for Montgomery. "Listen, if you want to get to the big leagues, watch me," he told Stengel.

Elberfeld taught Stengel the tactics, strategies and tricks of inside baseball. He coached him on hitting behind the runner to make the hit-and-run play work. Elberfeld showed Stengel how to get on base when it was most crucial: how to crowd the plate so he would be likely to get hit by a pitch—and how to put on an act, throwing his bat at the pitcher, cursing him, and taking a step or two toward the mound so the umpire wouldn't call him for intentionally getting hit.

Stengel made the big leagues late that season, joining the Brooklyn Dodgers. It was 1912: Ebbets Field was just being built. Ty Cobb was in his prime, batting .410 to win his sixth of nine consecutive AL batting championships. Babe Ruth, five years *younger* than Stengel, hadn't yet broken into baseball. The Yankees were still nine years away from their first pennant and 11 years away from moving into Yankee Stadium. The baseball heroes of New York were pitcher Christy Mathewson and manager John McGraw of the New York Giants.

Stengel played 17 games for the Dodgers in 1912. A left-handed batter, he hit .351 against right-handed pitchers and .250 against southpaws. By 1914 Stengel was a platooned outfielder, playing against right-handed pitch-

Outfielder Cliff Mapes (crashing into White Sox catcher Birdie Tebbetts) was another member of Stengel's platoon corps, and like most of the others, he didn't care for its commanding officer. "It's no secret Casey and I didn't get along," said Mapes, who in 1950 hit 12 homers and drove in 61 runs in just 356 at-bats. "I didn't like platoon baseball."

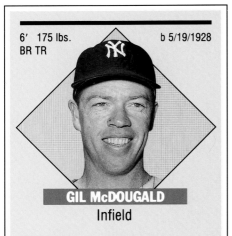

6' 175 lbs.
BR TR

b 5/19/1928

GIL McDOUGALD
Infield

When something of major importance happened in baseball in the 1950s, odds are Gil McDougald was there.

He played in eight World Series in his ten-year career at second, third and shortstop for Casey Stengel's platoon-happy Yankees. McDougald hit .306 and was named Rookie of the Year in 1951, then became the only rookie ever to hit a grand slam in the World Series. The slam came with the Series tied, two games all, and with a 1–1 score in Game 5, and spurred the Yanks to a six-game win.

McDougald's solid bat and versatile glove continued to be key to the Yankees' success, and he continued to find the spotlight. In Game 7 of the 1955 Series, he was doubled up when Sandy Amoros made a great catch to save Brooklyn's 2–0 win. In the 1956 Series he helped save Don Larsen's perfect game when he nailed Jackie Robinson by a step after Robinson's liner ricocheted off third baseman Andy Carey's glove toward McDougald at short.

In 1957 McDougald's roller coaster ride bottomed out when he hit a line drive that shattered the left eye and career of Herb Score, the Indians' brilliant young pitcher. Stengel said that McDougald was never the same after that, but he did rebound in 1958 to drive in the winning run in the All-Star Game, then wrapped up the season hitting .321 with two homers and four RBI as the Yanks battled back from a 3–1 deficit to defeat Milwaukee in the World Series.

Known as a clown, in 1923 Stengel showed he could also be dead serious when he charged the mound after the Phillies' Lefty Weinert threw a few pitches in tight. After the fight Stengel was escorted off the field by police.

ers only. He hit .316 and believed he should be playing every day—the lament of every platooned ballplayer. "They said I couldn't hit left-handers, and they'd pull me out as soon as a left-hander appeared," Stengel said. "But how was I expected to hit them when I never faced them?"

Platooning had already been around a while by that time. Credit for the practice goes to Ned Hanlon, who gained fame as "Foxy Ned," inventor of the hit-and-run play, who managed three straight championship Baltimore Oriole teams from 1894 to 1896, and who led the Brooklyn Dodgers to pennants in 1899 and 1900. In 1889 Hanlon, an outfielder with Pittsburgh, was named player-manager of the team. Major league teams carried only about a dozen players then, so platooning was hardly practical. Nevertheless, Hanlon had one left-handed-hitting outfielder who could not hit left-handed pitching, and the manager decided to bench him against lefties. The player was Hanlon himself—a case of invention by humility.

Rosters stayed small during the early years of the 20th century, so platooning was impractical except in unusual circumstances. Besides, baseball, then as now, was influenced by tradition, and the traditional managing approach was to play a set lineup. Tris Speaker, a great center fielder and a superb hitter against any kind of pitching, broke the mold in 1920 as player-manager of the Cleveland Indians. In left field he platooned Joe Evans, a right-handed batter, with Charlie Jamieson, a lefty. In right field he platooned former pitching star Joe Wood, a right-hander, with lefty Elmer Smith. Jack Graney, another left-handed hitter, was also worked in and out of the outfield. All this shuffling worked: the Indians edged the White Sox and Yankees for the pennant and beat the Dodgers in the World Series.

Stengel's first season as manager of the
Boston Braves—1938—was his best. The
team finished two games over .500, and
Stengel (above, far right) had a strong
starting staff, which led the NL with 83
complete games.

As other teams began to platoon more, traditionalists were outraged.
Ban Johnson, president of the American League, suggested that substitu-
tions be limited. Baseball writer John B. Sheridan wrote that Johnson was
"absolutely right in his contention that the constant substitution of players in
the championship games is unwise and has gone to such lengths that it has
become an abuse which threatens the popularity of the game and the impair-
ment of its dignity."

But dignity doesn't win pennants. John McGraw, a ferociously un-
dignified manager, became a highly sophisticated platooner, and one of his
best platoon players was Casey Stengel. In July 1921 Stengel was traded
from the Philadelphia Phillies to the Giants—from the worst team in the
league to the best. It was a big break—an opportunity to learn from the great
McGraw, who had already won six pennants and was widely regarded as a
strategic mastermind and an astute handler of men. Stengel sat on the Giants
bench that season and absorbed baseball wisdom from McGraw as the
Giants came from behind to win the pennant and went on to beat the Yankees
in the World Series.

In 1922 Stengel didn't get into a game until the season was six
weeks old. McGraw gave Stengel a chance only after two other outfielders
were shelved with injuries. Batting mostly against opposing right-handed
pitchers, Stengel lit up the league, batting .368 to lead a lineup that boasted
eight .300 hitters. The Giants won another world championship, and in 1923
the veteran Stengel—again platooned—hit .339 as the Giants won their third
straight pennant.

McGraw appreciated Stengel's intelligence and used him as an unofficial
coach who instructed young players and sometimes coached first base during

Continued on page 170

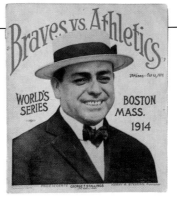

George Stallings

The Boston Braves opened the 1914 season by losing 18 of their first 24 games. On July 15 they were in last place. Few were surprised. The Braves had finished last every season from 1909 through 1912. A new manager, George Tweedy Stallings, had lifted them to fifth place in 1913, and in the off-season they had picked up Johnny Evers, a star second baseman. Still, last place looked like a natural home for the Braves.

Not to Stallings. He had managed well, though without winning a pennant, in previous stints with three other major league teams. Stallings thought that the Braves could win in 1914 and said so. A tyrannical disciplinarian, he cursed and drove his players. They responded by winning 61 of their last 77 games to take the National League pennant by 10½ games, then swept the favored Athletics in the World Series.

The team earned an enduring nickname—"the Miracle Braves"—and Stallings got a nickname any manager would covet—"the Miracle Man." He never won another pennant, but he remains one of baseball's most legendary managers.

Stallings was smart. He may have been the first NL manager to platoon extensively, and his platooning made the most of a deep but mediocre crew of outfielders. He used his pitchers skillfully—and, in 1914, with a little luck. Bill James went 26–7 with an ERA of 1.90 and beat the Athletics in two Series games—but then James could muster only 11 more wins the rest of his career.

Boston catcher Hank Gowdy said he admired the way Stallings could chew out a player, raising invective to an art form. Stallings wasn't loved, but he was respected. "No matter how you felt," said infielder Red Smith, "you had to admit that nobody knew more baseball. And nobody ever brought him up speechless."

Even if he had never won, Stallings would be remembered for a quote that binds all managers, and for his extraordinarily superstitious behavior. The quote came after he had retired to his Georgia plantation. A doctor told him he had a bad heart and then asked what might have caused it. "Bases on balls, you so-and-so, bases on balls," Stallings replied.

Stallings' superstitions were confounding, because he was an educated man and the son of a Confederate general. He attended Virginia Military Institute and The Johns Hopkins University, aiming, until baseball intervened, to become a doctor. Off the field he dressed well and behaved in courtly fashion. On the field he was enslaved by superstition. He couldn't stand to see scraps of paper; opposing players soon learned to bedevil him with litter. He credited some of the Braves' success in 1914 to a lucky dime, given to him by a friend from Havana who said it had been blessed by the Cuban pope. He carried a rabbit's foot, rubbed it for luck until the fur was gone—and kept rubbing it.

When his team got a hit, Stallings would remain frozen in position until the next out; he considered it good luck. During the 1914 pennant drive, Stallings was bent double, tying a shoelace, when a Brave singled. He stayed there, in agony, as Brave after Brave reached base safely—ten straight hits. When the rally finally ended, two players had to help him straighten up.

Stallings played only seven games in the major leagues, won only one pennant in 13 years of managing and wound up with a losing record. But because of the Braves' improbable success in 1914, Stallings is still remembered as "the Miracle Man."

GEORGE STALLINGS

Manager
Philadelphia Phillies 1897-1898
Detroit Tigers 1901
New York Highlanders 1909-1910
Boston Braves 1913-1920

GAMES		**1,813**
WINS		
Career		**879**
Season High		**94**
LOSSES		
Career		**898**
Season High		**90**
WINNING PERCENTAGE		
Career		**.495**
Season High		**.614**
PENNANT		**1914**
WORLD CHAMPIONSHIP		**1914**

According to historian Bill James, George Stallings (above) was the first manager "who formulated the idea of platooning as a weapon, rather than as a possible response to a player's weakness." Still, Stallings (left, center) would have been lost in 1914 without pitchers Bill James (left) and Dick Rudolph (right), who combined for 53 wins.

games. McGraw and Stengel talked baseball for hours, deep into the night, in
the kitchen of McGraw's suburban home. McGraw saw in Stengel a baseball
intelligence that was obscured, in the eyes of most observers, by Casey's wit
and clowning.

Stengel was *funny,* and he loved to ham it up. He entertained fans with
pantomime routines and swapped wisecracks with box-seat patrons. As a
Dodger, he was a favorite with fans at Brooklyn's Ebbets Field. Traded to
the Pirates, Stengel and his new teammates came to Brooklyn for a series in
1919. Stengel was not hitting well, and the Brooklyn fans good-naturedly
jeered him as he came to bat, shouting, "One out!" He lifted his cap to the
crowd after making a difficult catch, but took an earful of cheerful jeering
when he subsequently let a tough hit get by him, allowing three runs to score.

Stengel was playing right field that day. As was the custom in Ebbets
Field, he often sat in the bullpen, located in foul ground near right field, when
the Pirates came up to bat, rather than walk all the way to the visitors'
dugout. A pitcher somehow grabbed a sparrow that hopped nearby. "Let me
have it," Stengel said. He covered it with his cap, and as his turn to bat approached he trotted to the dugout. Just before walking to the plate, he put on
the cap. The crowd again greeted Casey with cheerful boos, whereupon he
turned to the stands, bowed and doffed his cap—literally giving the patrons
the bird, which fluttered away.

With the Phillies one spring, Stengel hatched an act to entertain
fans in Fort Wayne, Indiana, where the Phils were playing an exhibition
game. A good-sized crowd was on hand for batting practice, including a man
in overalls and a straw hat who loudly ridiculed the Phillie players. Finally,
a player challenged the rube, inviting him to take a few swings himself. To

Bullet Bob Turley (19, with Stengel and catcher Elston Howard) was the Yankees' main man in 1958. He went 21-7 with a league-high 19 complete games, then played a huge role in the World Series against Milwaukee as the Yankees became the first team ever to come back from a 3-1 deficit and win. Turley tossed a five-hit shutout in Game 5, saved Game 6 by getting the last out with the tying run on third, and won Game 7 with 6⅔ innings of two-hit relief.

the fans' surprise, the yokel hit the ball hard: line drives, long fly balls, home runs. It was Stengel, having a good time and giving the fans their money's worth.

By the time the Giants won their fourth straight pennant in 1924, Stengel had been traded to the Braves. He was about washed up as a player and about ready to show his stuff as a manager. In 1925 the Braves made him player-manager of their minor league affiliate, Worcester, Massachusetts, of the Eastern League. He tripled as president of the shoestring operation. Stengel had a good year, hitting .320 and leading Worcester from last place to third, and he became friendly with George Weiss, general manager of New Haven in the same league. When their teams were in the same town, Stengel and Weiss—like Stengel and McGraw a few years before—sat up late, talking baseball.

The Toledo Mud Hens, a Giant farm club in a higher-ranking league, needed a new manager for 1926. McGraw recommended Stengel, who wanted the job but was still under contract to the Braves' team. The situation called for Stengelese action, and Casey rose to the occasion. Acting as the team's president, he released himself as a player, fired himself as manager and resigned as president, freeing himself to sign with Toledo as manager.

Stengel managed Toledo for six years, winning one pennant. He established a reputation as a strategist, an umpire baiter and a taskmaster, yet still found opportunities to clown. The Depression threw the Mud Hens into receivership. In 1932 Stengel hired on as a coach for the Brooklyn Dodgers, and in 1934 he was promoted to manager. The Dodgers finished sixth, but Stengel had the satisfaction of beating the Giants the final two days of the

1927

In 1927 Stengel (middle row, fourth from right) was in his second year as manager of the Toledo Mud Hens. His team included some former major league stars, including shortstop Everett Scott (front row, far right), who played in 1,307 consecutive major league games; Jesse Barnes (front row, second from left), a 25-game winner for the Giants in 1919; and Rosy Ryan (middle row, far right), who led the league in shutouts for the world champion Giants in 1921 and 1922.

1934 season, allowing the St. Louis Cardinals' "Gashouse Gang" to squeeze past and win the pennant.

The Dodgers had been known for years as the "Daffiness Boys," because they often pulled boneheaded plays. The most famous occurred in 1926 when Babe Herman attempted to stretch a double, only to find two other Dodgers occupying third base. Stengel's clowning burnished the Brooklyn image. Like many managers of his day, he coached third base. The Dodgers had an outfielder named Nick Tremark who stood only 5′ 5″, and when he got on first base, Stengel looked for him through make-believe binoculars. The crowd loved it.

Stengel was an avid teacher, helping his young players learn the game. His catcher was Al Lopez, who later managed the Cleveland Indians to a pennant in 1954 and the Chicago White Sox to a pennant in 1959—the only seasons among Stengel's 12 years as Yankee manager that his team *didn't* win the pennant. Someone once mentioned to Stengel that Lopez was a smart manager. "Sure he's smart," Stengel replied. "I taught him, didn't I?"

But Stengel wasn't just teaching. He was learning—clowning and coaching and managing his way through a 39-year undergraduate education until he got the Yankee managership. He had long suffered the frustrations of the second-division damned. While Stengel was managing the Boston Braves, one of his players popped up with runners on second and third. Mad at himself, the player was still near home plate when the next batter took a wild pitch. The Boston runner on third broke for home. His disconsolate teammate, unaware of what was going on, picked up the loose ball and tossed

When Stengel took over as manager of the Brooklyn Dodgers in 1934, he inherited hard-throwing, hard-drinking right-hander Van Lingle Mungo. Mungo led the majors with 315⅓ innings pitched that season, and not many of them were quick, as he gave up 300 hits, walked 108 and struck out 184.

In 11 full seasons with Stengel's Yankees, outfielder Hank Bauer cashed nine World Series checks—seven of them winners' shares. He returned to the World Series as manager of the 1966 Baltimore Orioles, and cashed another winners' share as the Orioles swept the Los Angeles Dodgers.

it to the opposing catcher, who tagged out the runner. Realizing his stupidity, the poor Boston player walked up and down the dugout with his head down, whereupon a line-drive foul skulled him. "Don't touch him!" yelled Stengel. "Leave him lay there. It might drive some sense into the son of a bitch."

Back in the minors after six years with the Braves, Stengel managed the Milwaukee Brewers to an American Association pennant and the Oakland Oaks to a Pacific Coast League pennant. He drank a lot and talked a lot, but he was not a drunk and he talked about little other than baseball. "I don't play cards, I don't play golf, and I don't go to the picture show," Stengel said. "All that's left is baseball." George Weiss, Stengel's friend from their minor league days, was a front-office man with the same kind of tunnel vision, and he became general manager of the Yankees just in time to hire Stengel to manage the Yanks for 1949. By that time, Stengel had been managing for most of the previous 24 seasons after playing for 16. He was introduced to the New York press on October 12, 1948—25 years to the day after he hit his second game-winning homer of the 1923 World Series.

Even without DiMaggio and Keller, the Yankees got off to a fast start in 1949. Belying his 59 years, Stengel was an alert, lively manager, pacing the dugout, yelling encouragement to his players and giving them advice, whether they wanted it or not. Like Baltimore's Earl Weaver in later years, he demonstrated a knack for using every player on the roster, taking advantage of a player's strengths and benching him in situations likely to expose his weaknesses.

His platooning ruffled the feathers of proud Yankee players, but Stengel played to win, day by day, without deferring to the feelings of his men. He

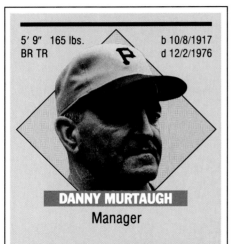

| 5' 9" 165 lbs. | b 10/8/1917 |
| BR TR | d 12/2/1976 |

DANNY MURTAUGH
Manager

For 20 years, whenever the Pittsburgh Pirates needed a boost, they called Danny Murtaugh. The genial, witty Irishman was hired to manage the club on four separate occasions. But when he first got the job, in August 1957 —after a lackluster nine-year career as a major league second baseman—it was only a temporary position, and the Pirates were lousy. They hadn't had a winning season since 1948 and had finished last five times in seven years. But the Pirate lineup included future stars Bill Mazeroski, Dick Groat and Roberto Clemente, and under Murtaugh they went 26–25. The next season, 1958, they finished second, and in 1960 Murtaugh presided over the most unlikely World Series win ever, as the Bucs were outscored 55–27 by the Yankees but won the title on Mazeroski's homer in Game 7.

Poor health sidelined Murtaugh after the 1964 season, but he returned for a short stint in 1967, then was back full-time in 1970. He led the Pirates to two straight division titles, and in 1971 they came back from being down 2–0 in the World Series to beat the Orioles in seven. A heart condition convinced him that he should retire—again—at the end of the 1971 season, but in late 1973 he was back and led the Pirates to two more NL East titles in 1974 and 1975. Two months after guiding the Bucs to second place in 1976, Murtaugh, one of the most respected and well-liked managers of his time, died in his hometown of Chester, Pennsylvania.

Second baseman Jerry Coleman (above, forcing Chicago's Fred Hancock) just hit .263 lifetime, but played a key role on six world championship teams. "He's only a one-for-four hitter," someone said of Coleman. "But that one hit will beat you."

got the most static from Gene Woodling, up from a .385 season in the Pacific Coast League, and Hank Bauer, an ex-Marine whom one sportswriter described as a man with "a face like a clenched fist." Stengel sometimes went against the percentages, playing the right-handed Bauer against a righty pitcher, or Woodling against a lefty; it depended on who Stengel thought could do the better job that day. On one such occasion Bauer started, got three straight hits off a right-handed pitcher—and then was pulled in favor of Woodling when the opposing manager put in a left-hander. Both players were angry, and after the game Stengel called them into his office. "I don't give a good goddamn what you call me," Stengel told Bauer. "You can call me a crazy old man, and maybe I am. But it's my team and I'm going to run it my way. Now I'm going to tell you why I pulled you. You got your three hits, right? So let me tell you something, Mr. Bauer. You're not a one-thousand hitter. And you're not a five-hundred hitter. In fact, Mr. Bauer, you're not even a three-thirty-three hitter. So you had your three hits for the day and that's all it was going to be. That was your quota. I didn't think you had any more hits in you." Stengel turned to Woodling. "The same goes for you," he said. "so forget all this old-man crap and play your position and do whatever the hell I tell you." Bauer and Woodling didn't like it, but they had no choice but to comply—and Stengel kept platooning them, season after season.

He also kept winning. Stengel was a strategic innovator. He was the first manager to use his top relief pitcher so often and in such crucial situations that the "stopper" became a star. Southpaw Joe Page, an overpowering fastball pitcher, filled that role in 1949 with 13 wins and 27 saves. Stengel often brought in Page in the eighth or ninth, *before* his starting pitcher tired—

standard practice today but unusual in Stengel's era. In contrast to today's conventional wisdom, Stengel did not limit his stopper to late-game duty. He believed in stopping an opposing rally that might break open the game, no matter what the inning.

DiMaggio's dramatic return at the end of June helped lift the Yankees into the 1949 pennant race. With two games to go, the Red Sox led the Yankees by one game—and, by a happy scheduling coincidence, they came to Yankee Stadium for the last two games of the season.

In the first game, Allie Reynolds, the Yankee starter, was off his form, so Stengel brought on Page in the third inning. He started poorly, walking in two runs, but settled into a groove and blanked Boston the rest of the way. The Yankees came from behind to win, tying the race, and they beat Boston the next day to win the pennant.

Throughout his career, Stengel was equally inventive in his use of pinch hitters. When he saw an opportunity to win a game with a rally, he went to his bench, whether it was the ninth inning or the third. Infielders were often insulted when pulled in the early innings, but Stengel didn't care. After all, he believed in using his bench—in using a young Billy Martin or Jerry Coleman or Gil McDougald. "I wish I didn't have so many green peas, but I can't win with my old men," Stengel said. "We have to rebuild." Al Lopez, who was Stengel's constant rival in AL pennant races, said Stengel's success resulted partly from his willingness to play his youngsters. "He took chances with kids and he won with them," Lopez said. "Casey would sit and talk to them by the hour. He never had any children of his own, so he had a lot to give them."

Continued on page 178

The Yankees didn't exactly steamroll the Phillies in the 1950 World Series. Instead, they used great pitching, timely hitting and solid defense to sweep the NL champs. In the eighth inning of Game 2 (above) second baseman Jerry Coleman helped turn a 5-4-3 double play to end the inning, and the Yanks won it in the tenth on a homer by Joe DiMaggio.

Al Lopez

The 1950s were not good years for Yankee haters. Without Al Lopez the decade would have been even worse. If not for Lopez, one of the best liked and most respected managers in recent baseball history, Casey Stengel's Yankees would have won every American League pennant between 1949 and 1964. Only Lopez' 1954 Cleveland Indians and his 1959 Chicago White Sox prevented total Yankee dominance.

Lopez was a rarity—a first-rate ballplayer who became a first-rate manager. Until Bob Boone broke his record in 1987, no one had ever caught more games than Lopez—a total of 1,918 with Brooklyn, Boston, Pittsburgh and Cleveland—and he attributed his knowledge of the game to all the time he spent watching every move on the field in front of him. Not surprisingly, he was an expert handler of pitchers, and both of his championship teams had outstanding staffs. The 1954 Indians, who won an AL-record 111 games, had one of the best starting rotations of all time: Bob Lemon, Early Wynn, Mike Garcia and an aging but still effective Bob Feller. Lopez was smart enough not to juggle the rotation once it had been set, and that stability helped keep the Indians' pitchers in a season-long groove. Often he would allow them to decide when they wanted to come out of a game. And time after time they held opponents in check until one of the team's sluggers—Vic Wertz, Al Rosen or Larry Doby—knocked one out of the park.

The 1959 White Sox were built around an entirely different style, and their success was a testament to Lopez' flexibility. They had pitching, speed and defense, but no power and had to constantly scramble for runs. Typically, their attack would revolve around singles, sacrifices and stolen bases, usually by Luis Aparicio. "A typical White Sox rally consisted of two bloopers, an error, a passed ball, a couple of bases on balls, and, as a final crusher, a hit batsman," wrote team owner Bill Veeck. "Never did a team make less use of a lively ball." Still, the "Go-Go" Sox won 35 games by a mere one run and a lot of the credit had to go to Lopez for his masterful management of the popgun offense.

A key was his ability to squeeze every drop of talent from his bench players. "They're the guys you have to worry about," he said. "You have to keep them in a good frame of mind."

Veeck once said that if Lopez had a weakness, it was that he was "too decent." But Lopez was a nice guy who never came close to finishing last. Only once did a Lopez team finish in the second division, and that was late in his career, after he had been coaxed out of retirement to manage the 1968 White Sox. In his 17 years of leading the Indians and White Sox, his teams finished either first or second 12 times.

Health problems forced Lopez to retire for good early in the 1969 season. By then he had managed teams to 1,410 wins. "I guess the biggest secret to being a successful manager," he once said, "is to have discipline on the team. You have to respect the players and the players have to respect you." But Lopez didn't have to worry about the latter; with patience, rather than temper tantrums, he won over his players and never lost control of his teams.

AL LOPEZ

Manager
Cleveland Indians 1951-1956
Chicago White Sox 1958-1965,
1968-1969
Hall of Fame 1977

GAMES	**2,425**
WINS	
Career	**1,410**
Season High *(2nd all time)*	**111**
LOSSES	
Career	**1,004**
Season High	**77**
WINNING PERCENTAGE	
Career *(8th all time)*	**.584**
Season High *(3rd all time)*	**.721**
PENNANTS	**1954, 1959**

No matter what dugout he was in, Al Lopez (top, right, with Red Ruffing, left, with reporters after a White Sox win) was without doubt a player's manager. "It's not too difficult to earn their respect," he said. "All you have to do is treat them the way you wanted to be treated when you were a player."

Second baseman Billy Martin turned his game up a notch for the World Series. A .257 lifetime hitter, Martin hit .333 with five homers—and committed just one error—in his five World Series. "I remember everything about every World Series game I played," he said.

Stengel was just as wise in his use of veterans. With George Weiss' help, Stengel made sure he had the right men ready to come off the bench. The Yankees became famous—or notorious—for picking up fading stars from the NL who still had enough pop in their bats or arms to win games. The Yanks picked up slugger Johnny Mize in 1949, first baseman Johnny Hopp in 1950, pitcher Johnny Sain in 1951, reliever Jim Konstanty in 1954, outfielder Enos Slaughter in 1954 and again in 1956, and pitcher Sal Maglie in 1957. Stengel used them judiciously, and they all contributed to Yankee pennants. When the Yankees first acquired Slaughter, the old Cardinal war-horse told Stengel that he expected to play every day. "My boy," said the 65-year-old Stengel to the 38-year-old Slaughter, "you play when I tell you and you'll stay up here a long time."

Stengel liked versatile players who could, to use baseball vernacular, "execute." For example, he liked Gil McDougald, who played second, short and third equally well, hit well and with decent power, and could push a ground ball to second base or bunt to advance a runner. As Casey put it in his confounding way, McDougald was "a very awkward man, a wonderful man." Not that Stengel treated him kindly. McDougald had an odd batting stance, and pitchers learned that they could get him out by throwing to the outside corner. McDougald resisted change until Stengel moved from advice to command. "You, I want you to change that horseshit stance of yours," Stengel snapped. "I don't care how you change it. Just change it, and I mean now." Reluctantly, McDougald changed it—and his batting average rose 50 points.

In 1951 Stengel's only regulars were Yogi Berra and Phil Rizzuto. To get more hitting, Stengel benched second baseman Jerry Coleman, played McDougald at second base and started Bobby Brown—good hit, poor field

—at third. To protect a lead, he often pulled Brown, moved McDougald to third, and put in Coleman or Martin at second. The Yankees had three first basemen that year, all left-handed: veterans Johnny Mize and Johnny Hopp, and young Joe Collins, who also played the outfield. Stengel nevertheless found useful ways to rotate them. DiMaggio was aging, so Stengel moved him and the other outfielders—Woodling, Bauer, Cliff Mapes, Joe Collins, and a couple of promising youngsters named Jackie Jensen and Mickey Mantle—in and out of the lineup.

Stengel's system had a makeshift look about it, but baseball observers gradually came to realize that Casey wasn't dumb, no matter how obscurely he described his strategies. "If you've got a number of good men setting around on the bench you'll do yourself a favor playing them, because every time one of my front players got hurt I noticed the fella I stuck in his place would bust out with hits," Stengel explained. "Then just about the time he slowed down he'd oblige me by stepping in a hole and another fella would take his place and hit. I decided I'd never count on one player taking care of one position for an entire season. If you've got two or three men who can't play anyplace else pretty soon you're gonna run out of room for pitchers, and that's why you've got to have players who can do more than one thing." Got it?

Sometimes Stengel confounded everyone—even his friend and rival, Lopez. "I swear, I don't understand some of the things he does when he manages," Lopez once said. "I've tried to figure them out, but they just don't make sense." In Game 6, the last game of the 1951 World Series, the Yanks took a 4–1 lead into the ninth inning. The Giants loaded the bases on three singles, and Stengel yanked right-hander Johnny Sain

The Yankees (above) were jubilant after beating the Red Sox, 5-3, to clinch the 1949 pennant on the season's final day. Three years later former Boston Braves starter Johnny Sain (below) added his baffling assortment of pitches to Stengel's staff.

Stengel's lineup card got a workout in the
1955 World Series against Brooklyn. Stengel
used eight different pinch-hitters—including
pitcher Tommy Byrne—in the Series, but
ran out of magic in Game 7, as the
Dodgers' Johnny Podres tossed an eight-hit
shutout.

Al Lopez played for Stengel in Brooklyn and Boston in the 1930s, then wound up as Stengel's rival with the White Sox and Indians in the 1950s. But the rivalry never endangered what was a great friendship. "Casey was great with young players," Lopez said. "He loved to teach."

in favor of journeyman reliever Bob Kuzava, a southpaw, even though the next two Giant hitters were right-handed and very dangerous. Monte Irvin, the NL's RBI champion, flied deep to left, scoring the runner from third and advancing the other two runners. Bobby Thomson, who had won the pennant for the Giants with his "shot heard 'round the world" homer, also flied deep to left; a second run scored. Sal Yvars, a .317 hitter and another right-hander, sliced a hard line drive to Bauer in right field. All three hit the ball hard, but Stengel's strategy had somehow worked, and the Yankees were world champions again.

The next fall Stengel tempted fate again—this time at Ebbets Field, where the Dodgers' home run power posed a constant risk. The World Series was tied at three games each. The Yanks took a 4–2 lead in Game 7, but in the last of the seventh the Dodgers loaded the bases with one out. Again, Stengel called in Kuzava, this time to face Duke Snider, a left-handed slugger, and Jackie Robinson, who batted right. Walking from the bullpen to the mound, Kuzava himself wondered about Stengel. "This guy has got to be crazy to bring me in here," he thought. But he retired Snider on a pop fly to third and Robinson on a pop near the mound that second baseman Billy Martin caught. Kuzava retired Brooklyn in the final two innings, and the Yankees had yet another world championship.

Stengel played the percentages wisely, not blindly. He rarely called for bunts, because they were likely to donate an out to the opposition. He didn't like to pull the infield in to cut off a run: "Playing your infield in turns a .200 hitter into a .300 hitter," he said. He drilled his infielders hard on the double play. "It's two-thirds of an inning!" he explained. He admired pitchers like Eddie Lopat, who coaxed hitters into hitting ground balls. "Throw those

sinkers," Stengel said. "Make 'em hit ground balls. Never heard anyone getting home runs on ground balls."

Looking back, it is shocking to discover that in Stengel's first four seasons, the Yankees were *never* favored to win the pennant. To be sure, Stengel had strong teams. But so did Cleveland, Detroit and Boston. The Yanks edged the Red Sox by one game in 1949, the Tigers by three in 1950, the Indians by five in 1951 and the Indians by two in 1952. Those were close races, the kind in which the manager makes a difference. In 1953 the Yanks were finally favored, won their fifth straight pennant and beat the Dodgers for their fifth straight world championship.

Stengel's Yankee dynasty paralleled the rise of television, and his wrinkled face and tangled syntax made him a natural for the medium. Critics disparaged him as a clown—they always had—and as he got older he became more garrulous and less patient with young players. Still, he won five more pennants: the final one came in 1960, whereupon the Yankees fired him on the grounds that, at 70, he was too old. "I commenced winning pennants as soon as I got here, but I did not commence getting any younger," Stengel explained. He signed on to manage the brand-new New York Mets, a team so dreadful that no manager could win with them. He managed the Mets for four seasons—they finished dead last each time—and then retired.

When Stengel was 83, a reporter asked him how he had achieved his managing success. "I was a platoon manager, and McGraw platooned me, so if he platooned me I found out he was right," Stengel said. It wasn't that simple: Stengel was much more than a protégé of John McGraw. But if you needed an epitaph for the old man you could do worse than to write, "Casey Stengel, the Great Platoon Manager." ◗

Stengel came out of retirement to manage the expansion Mets in 1962, and watched as his career won-loss record took a pounding. His 3½ seasons with the Mets dropped his winning percentage from .546 to .508.

Ultimately, managers are helpless. They can't go out and play the game, so sometimes they must sit and watch it all fall apart. No one had a more painful vigil than the Phillies' Gene Mauch, who in 1964 watched as his team's 6½-game lead evaporated in just seven long, late September days. And although he was considered by many to be one of the game's best strategic minds, Mauch never made it to a World Series in 26 years as a manager.

MOST YEARS

1. Connie Mack	53	1894-1896	PIT NL	
		1901-1950	PHI AL	
2. John McGraw	33	1899	BAL NL	
		1901-1902	BAL AL	
		1902-1932	NY NL	
3. Bucky Harris	29	1924-1928	WAS AL	
		1929-1933	DET AL	
		1934	BOS AL	
		1935-1942	WAS AL	
		1943	PHI NL	
		1947-1948	NY AL	
		1950-1954	WAS AL	
		1955-1956	DET AL	
4. Gene Mauch	26	1960-1968	PHI NL	
		1969-1975	MON NL	
		1976-1980	MIN AL	
		1981-1982	CAL AL	
		1985-1987	CAL AL	

5. Bill McKechnie	25	1915	NWK FL	
		1922-1926	PIT NL	
		1928-1929	StL NL	
		1930-1937	BOS NL	
		1938-1946	CIN NL	
− Casey Stengel	25	1934-1936	BKN NL	
		1938-1943	BOS NL	
		1949-1960	NY AL	
		1962-1965	NY NL	
7. Joe McCarthy	24	1926-1930	CHI NL	
		1931-1946	NY AL	
		1948-1950	BOS AL	
− Leo Durocher	24	1939-1946, 1948	BKN NL	
		1948-1955	NY NL	
		1966-1972	CHI NL	
		1972-1973	HOU NL	
9. Walter Alston	23	1954-1957	BKN NL	
		1958-1976	LA NL	
10. Jimmy Dykes	21	1934-1946	CHI AL	
		1951-1953	PHI AL	
		1954	BAL AL	
		1958	CIN NL	
		1959-1960	DET AL	
		1960-1961	CLE AL	
− Sparky Anderson*	21	1970-1978	CIN NL	
		1979-1990	DET AL	

* Active manager as of end of 1990 season.

MOST GAMES

1. Connie Mack   7,755
2. John McGraw   4,801
3. Bucky Harris   4,408
4. Gene Mauch   3,942
5. Casey Stengel   3,766
6. Leo Durocher   3,739
7. Walter Alston   3,658
8. Bill McKechnie   3,651
9. Joe McCarthy   3,487
10. Sparky Anderson*   3,285

Ralph Houk

MOST WINS

1. Connie Mack   3,731
2. John McGraw   2,784
3. Bucky Harris   2,157
4. Joe McCarthy   2,125
5. Walter Alston   2,040
6. Leo Durocher   2,008
7. Casey Stengel   1,905
8. Gene Mauch   1,902
9. Bill McKechnie   1,899
10. Sparky Anderson*   1,837

MOST LOSSES

1. Connie Mack   3,948
2. Bucky Harris   2,218
3. Gene Mauch   2,037
4. John McGraw   1,959
5. Casy Stengel   1,842
6. Bill McKechnie   1,724
7. Leo Durocher   1,709
8. Walter Alston   1,613
9. Jimmy Dykes   1,541
10. Ralph Houk   1,531

IT'S A GREAT SEASON FOR CONNIE MACK OF THE ATHLETICS AND HIS FAMOUS SCORE CARD

Connie Mack

HIGHEST WINNING PERCENTAGE

1. Joe McCarthy   .615
2. Jim Mutrie   .611
3. Charlie Comiskey   .608
4. Frank Selee   .598
5. Billy Southworth   .597
5. Frank Chance   .593
7. John McGraw   .587
8. Al Lopez   .584
9. Earl Weaver   .583
10. Cap Anson   .578

MOST LEAGUE CHAMPIONSHIP GAMES

1.	Whitey Herzog	30
–	Tommy Lasorda*	30
3.	Sparky Anderson*	27
4.	Earl Weaver	22
5.	Billy Martin	21
6.	Dick Williams	18
7.	Tony LaRussa*	17
8.	Danny Murtaugh	14
9.	Dick Howser	13
–	Davey Johnson	13

MOST WORLD SERIES GAMES

1.	Casey Stengel	63
2.	John McGraw	55
3.	Connie Mack	43
–	Joe McCarthy	43
5.	Walter Alston	40
6.	Miller Huggins	34
7.	Sparky Anderson*	28
8.	Dick Williams	26
9.	Earl Weaver	24
10.	Bill McKechnie	22

MOST LEAGUE CHAMPIONSHIP GAMES WON

1.	Sparky Anderson*	18
2.	Whitey Herzog	16
–	Tommy Lasorda	16
4.	Earl Weaver	15
5.	Tony LaRussa*	13
6.	Dick Williams	9
7.	Billy Martin	8
8.	Roger Craig	7
–	Davey Johnson	7
10.	Bob Lemon	6

MOST WORLD SERIES GAMES WON

1.	Casey Stengel	37
2.	Joe McCarthy	30
3.	John McGraw	26
4.	Connie Mack	24
5.	Walter Alston	20
6.	Miller Huggins	18
7.	Sparky Anderson*	16
8.	Dick Williams	12
9.	Bucky Harris	11
–	Earl Weaver	11

MOST LEAGUE CHAMPIONSHIP GAMES LOST

1.	Whitey Herzog	14
–	Tommy Lasorda*	14
3.	Billy Martin	13
4.	Danny Murtaugh	10
5.	Sparky Anderson*	9
–	Dick Howser	9
–	Danny Ozark	9
–	Dick Williams	9
9.	Joe Morgan*	8
10.	Gene Mauch	7
–	Earl Weaver	7

MOST WORLD SERIES GAMES LOST

1.	John McGraw	28
2.	Casey Stengel	26
3.	Walter Alston	20
4.	Connie Mack	19
5.	Miller Huggins	15
6.	Dick Williams	14
7.	Joe McCarthy	13
–	Earl Weaver	13
9.	Hughie Jennings	12
–	Charlie Grimm	12
–	Sparky Anderson*	12

* Active manager as of end of 1990 season.

PICTURE CREDITS

Front cover: Pirates' mound conference, 1982, by John W. McDonough.

Back cover: Roger Craig and Don Zimmer by Bryan Yablonsky.

Weaver's Way
4-5 Jerry Wachter; 6 Jerry Wachter; 7 National Baseball Library, Cooperstown, NY; 8 Tadder/Baltimore; 9(left) AP/Wide World Photos; 9(right) Jerry Wachter; 10(left) National Baseball Library, Cooperstown, NY; 10(right) Anthony Neste; 11 Walter Iooss, Jr.; 13(left) Manny Millan/*Sports Illustrated;* 13(right) Focus On Sports, Inc.; 14 Ron Menchine Collection/Renée Comet Photography; 15(top) National Baseball Library, Cooperstown, NY; 15(bottom) Ronald C. Modra/*Sports Illustrated;* 16 Tadder/Baltimore; 17 AP/Wide World Photos; 18 UPI/Bettmann Newsphotos; 19(left) James Drake/*Sports Illustrated;* 19(right) Jerry Wachter; 20(left) National Baseball Library, Cooperstown, NY; 20(right) Tony Triolo/*Sports Illustrated;* 21 UPI/Bettmann Newsphotos; 22 AP/Wide World Photos; 23 Nancy Hogue; 24 Bryan Yablonsky; 25(left) Ron Vesely; 25(right) John Iacono/*Sports Illustrated.*

Signals
26-27 Dick Raphael; 28 AP/Wide World Photos; 29 Bryan Yablonsky; 30(left) Ron Vesely; 30(right) Michael Ponzini; 31(left) Anthony Neste; 31(right) Anthony Neste; 32(top) Dick Raphael; 32(bottom four) Paul Jasienski; 33(top left) Paul Jasienski; 33(top right) Bruce L. Schwartzman; 33(bottom) Fred Kaplan; 34(left) Fred Kaplan; 34(right) Dick Raphael; 35 Dick Raphael; 36(left) National Baseball Library, Cooperstown, NY; 36(right) Bruce L. Schwartzman; 37 Paul Jasienski; 38 AP/Wide World Photos; 39(both) Mitchell B. Rebel/Sportschrome East/West; 40 John W. McDonough; 41 Anthony Neste; 42 AP/Wide World Photos; 43 Richard Mackson/*Sports Illustrated.*

Scientific Baseball
44 Heinz Kluetmeier/*Sports Illustrated;* 45 Ron Menchine Collection/Renée Comet Photography; 46 Brown Brothers; 47(left) Ron Menchine Collection/Renée Comet Photography; 47(right) National Baseball Library, Cooperstown, NY; 48 Nancy Hogue; 49 Brown Brothers; 50 Ron Menchine Collection/Renée Comet Photography; 51 Neil Leifer/*Sports Illustrated;* 52(left) National Baseball Library, Cooperstown, NY; 52(right) Lee Balterman; 53 Tony Tomsic; 54(left) National Baseball Library, Cooperstown, NY; 54(right) Boston Public Library; 55 Scott Halleran; 56 National Baseball Library, Cooperstown, NY; 57 National Baseball Library, Cooperstown, NY; 58 Ron Menchine Collection/Renée Comet Photography; 59 Brown Brothers; 60 UPI/Bettmann Newsphotos; 61(top) Ron Menchine Collection/Renée Comet Photography; 61(bottom) UPI/Bettmann Newsphotos.

The Babe's New Game
62 UPI/Bettmann Newsphotos; 63 Ron Menchine Collection/Renée Comet Photography; 64 UPI/Bettmann Newsphotos; 65 Bryan Yablonsky; 66 Ron Menchine Collection/Renée Comet Photography; 67(top) AP/Wide World Photos; 67(bottom) AP/Wide World Photos; 68(left) National Baseball Library, Cooperstown, NY; 68(right) Malcolm W. Emmons; 69(left) National Baseball Library, Cooperstown, NY; 69(right) Malcolm W. Emmons; 70 AP/Wide World Photos; 71 Dick Raphael; 72 Ron Menchine Collection/Renée Comet Photography; 73(left) FPG International; 73(right) National Baseball Library, Cooperstown, NY; 74 UPI/Bettmann Newsphotos; 75 National Baseball Library, Cooperstown, NY.

Cheating
76-77 AP/Wide World Photos; 78 AP/Wide World Photos; 79 Mel Bailey; 80 AP/Wide World Photos; 81(left) Mel Bailey; 81(right) Ron Menchine Collection/Renée Comet Photography; 82-83 AP/Wide World Photos; 84 National Baseball Library, Cooperstown, NY; 85 Photo by Joe Sebo; 86(left) Mitchell B. Rebel/Sportschrome East/West; 86(right) Malcolm W. Emmons; 87 AP/Wide World Photos; 88(left) AP/Wide World Photos; 88(right) Richard Darcey; 89 Bryan Yablonsky; 91(left) UPI/Bettmann Newsphotos; 91(right) Ron Vesely; 92 David Walberg; 93 AP/Wide World Photos.

Smart Moves
94 Marvin E. Newman; 95 Ron Menchine Collection/Renée Comet Photography; 96 AP/Wide World Photos; 97(left) Marvin E. Newman; 97(right) AP/Wide World Photos;

98(top) AP/Wide World Photos; 98(bottom) AP/Wide World Photos; 99 Ron Vesely; 100 Ron Menchine Collection/Renée Comet Photography; 101(top) AP/Wide World Photos; 101(bottom) UPI/Bettmann Newsphotos; 103 UPI/Bettmann Newsphotos; 104 UPI/Bettmann Newsphotos; 105 Ronald C. Modra; 106(top) Jeffrey E. Blackman; 106-107 Jeffrey E. Blackman; 107(top) Marvin E. Newman; 108(top left) Jeffrey E. Blackman; 108(top right) Bruce L. Schwartzman; 108(bottom left) Jeffrey E. Blackman; 108(bottom right) Ronald C. Modra; 109(top) Jeffrey E. Blackman; 109(bottom left) Scott Halleran; 109(bottom center) Bruce L. Schwartzman; 109(bottom right) James Drake/*Sports Illustrated.*

Masters of the Mound
110-111 Walter Iooss, Jr.; 112 AP/Wide World Photos; 113(left) Bryan Yablonsky; 113(right) UPI/Bettmann Newsphotos; 114(left) National Baseball Library, Cooperstown, NY; 114(right) AP/Wide World Photos; 115 Paul Jasienski; 116 Ron Menchine Collection/Renée Comet Photography; 117 The Bettmann Archive; 118(left) National Baseball Library, Cooperstown, NY; 118(right) AP/Wide World Photos; 119 Lewis Portnoy/Spectra/Action, Inc.; 120(left) AP/Wide World Photos; 120(right) Bruce L. Schwartzman; 121(left) Mitchell B. Rebel/Sportschrome East/West; 121(right) UPI/Bettmann Newsphotos; 123 Bruce L. Schwartzman; 124 Ron Menchine Collection/Renée Comet Photography; 125 UPI/Bettmann Newsphotos; 126 AP/Wide World Photos; 127 Brown Brothers.

Whiteyball
128-129 John Swart/Allsport USA; 130 Spectra-Action, Inc.; 131(left) Michael Ponzini; 131(right) UPI/Bettmann Newsphotos; 132 Michael Ponzini; 133 AP/Wide World Photos; 134(left) National Baseball Library, Cooperstown, NY; 134(right) AP/Wide World Photos; 135(left) Michael Ponzini; 135(right) UPI/Bettmann Newsphotos; 136 WOB Collection; 137(top) Anthony Neste; 137(bottom) Nancy Hogue; 138 Michael Ponzini; 139 Robert Riger; 140 David Walberg; 141 James Drake/*Sports Illustrated;* 142 WOB Collection; 143(top) Mel Bailey; 143(bottom) Ronald C. Modra.

Deception
144-145 AP/Wide World Photos; 146 Robert Riger; 147 Ronald C. Modra;

149(left) National Baseball Library, Cooperstown, NY; 149(right) Anthony Neste; 150 Ron Menchine Collection/Renée Comet Photography; 151(left) National Baseball Library, Cooperstown, NY; 151(right) The Bettmann Archive; 152(left) National Baseball Library, Cooperstown, NY; 152(right) AP/Wide World Photos; 153 New York *Daily News* Photo; 154 AP/Wide World Photos; 155 Ron Vesely; 156 WOB Collection; 157 UPI/Bettmann Newsphotos; 158 Bruce Schwartzman; 159 Malcolm W. Emmons.

Casey at the Helm
160 Neil Leifer; 161 Thomas Carwile Collection; 162(left) UPI/Bettmann Newsphotos; 162(right) Brown Brothers; 163 UPI/Bettmann Newsphotos; 164 AP/Wide World Photos; 165 AP/Wide World Photos; 166(left) AP/Wide World Photos; 166(right) National Baseball Library, Cooperstown, NY; 167 Brown Brothers; 168 Ron Menchine Collection/Renée Comet Photography; 169(top) National Baseball Library, Cooperstown, NY; 169(bottom) UPI/Bettmann Newsphotos; 170 AP/Wide World Photos; 171(left) AP/Wide World Photos; 171(right) Marvin E. Newman; 172 National Baseball Library, Cooperstown, NY; 173(left) David Scherman, *LIFE* Magazine © 1939 Time Warner Inc.; 173(right) Malcolm W. Emmons; 174(left) National Baseball Library, Cooperstown, NY; 174(right) AP/Wide World Photos; 175 UPI/Bettmann Newsphotos; 176 Ron Menchine Collection/Renée Comet Photography; 177(top) *The Sporting News;* 177(bottom left) *The Sporting News;* 177(bottom right) Ron Menchine Collection/Renée Comet Photography; 178 Robert Riger; 179(top) AP/Wide World Photos; 179(bottom) Ron Menchine Collection/Renée Comet Photography; 180 Walter Iooss, Jr.; 181(left) Carl Kidwiler Collection; 181(right) Marvin E. Newman; 182-183 Walter Iooss, Jr./*Sports Illustrated;* 184(both) Ron Menchine Collection/Renée Comet Photography; 185(top) AP/Wide World Photos; 185(bottom) Thomas Carwile Collection/Renée Comet Photography.

ACKNOWLEDGMENTS

The author and editors wish to thank:

Peter P. Clark, Tom Heitz, Bill Deane, Patricia Kelly, Dan Bennett, Frank Rollins and the staffs of the National Baseball Hall of Fame and the National Baseball Library, Cooperstown, New York; Nat Andriani, Wide World Photos, New York, New York; Renée Comet, Renée Comet Photography, Washington, D.C.; Joe Borras, Accokeek, Maryland; Dave Kelly, Library of Congress, Washington, D.C.; Karen Carpenter and Sunny Smith, *Sports Illustrated,* New York, New York; Ken Hancock, Alexandria, Virginia; John Holway, Alexandria, Virginia; Clarence "Lefty" Blasco, Van Nuys, California; Robert Harding and Ellen Hughes, National Museum of American History, Smithsonian Institution, Washington, D.C.; Helen Bowie Campbell and Gregory J. Schwalenberg, Babe Ruth Museum, Baltimore, Maryland; Stephen P. Gietschier, *The Sporting News.*

Illustrations: 102, 122, 138 by Jeff Dionise; 12, 48, 51, 85, 90 by Sam Ward

FOR FURTHER READING

Lawrence S. Ritter, *The Glory Of Their Times.* Macmillan, 1966.
Charles C. Alexander, *Ty Cobb.* Oxford, 1984.
Charles C. Alexander, *John McGraw.* Viking, 1988.
Donald Honig, *The Man In The Dugout.* Follett, 1977.
Whitey Herzog and Kevin Horrigan, *White Rat.* Harper & Row, 1987.
Earl Weaver with Terry Pluto, *Weaver On Strategy.* Macmillan, 1984.
Robert W. Creamer, *Stengel: His Life and Times.* Simon and Schuster, 1984.
Glen Waggoner, Kathleen Moloney and Hugh Howard, *Baseball By the Rules.* Taylor, 1987.
Ethan Allen, *Baseball Play and Strategy.* Krieger, 1982.
William Curran, *Big Sticks: The Batting Revolution of the Twenties.* Morrow, 1990.

World of Baseball is produced and
published by Redefinition, Inc.

WORLD OF BASEBALL

Editor	Glen B. Ruh
Design Director	Robert Barkin
Designer	Edwina Smith
Production Director	Irv Garfield
Senior Writer	Jonathan Kronstadt
Features Editor	Sharon Cygan
Text Editor	Carol Gardner
Staff Writer	Mark Lazen
Picture Editing	Rebecca Hirsh
	Louis P. Plummer
Design	Sue Pratt
	Collette Conconi
	Monique Strawderman
Copy Preparation	Anthony K. Pordes
	Ronald Stanley
Editorial Research	Janet Pooley
Index	Lynne Hobbs

REDEFINITION

Administration	Margaret M. Higgins
	June M. Nolan
Fulfillment Manager	Karen DeLisser Brown
Finance Director	Vaughn A. Meglan
PRESIDENT	Edward Brash

CONTRIBUTORS

Bill Mead is the author of *Baseball Goes To War*, *The Official New York Yankees Hater's Handbook*, *Two Spectacular Seasons*, and for World of Baseball *The Explosive Sixties* and *Low and Outside*. The closest he has come to the major leagues was as an eager participant in a Baltimore Orioles fantasy camp.

Henry Staat is Series Consultant for World of Baseball. A member of the Society for American Baseball Research since 1982, he helped initiate the concept for the series. He is an editor with Wadsworth, Inc., a publisher of college textbooks.

Ron Menchine, a sports advisor and collector, shared baseball material he has been collecting for 40 years. A radio sportscaster and sports director, he announced the last three seasons of the Washington Senators.

The editors also wish to thank the following writers for their contributions to this book: Randy Rieland, Washington, D.C.; John Ross, Washington, D.C.; Joann Stern, Washington, D.C.

Library of Congress Cataloging-in-Publication Data
The inside game/William B. Mead
  (World of Baseball)
includes index
  1. Baseball—United States—History.
  2. Baseball players—United States—Biography.
  I. Title. II. Series.
GV863.A1M433 1990   90–38508
796.357'0973—dc20
ISBN 0–924588–10–1

This book is one of a series that celebrates America's national pastime.

Redefinition also offers World of Baseball Top Ten Stat Finders.

For subscription information and prices, write:
  Customer Service, Redefinition Inc.
  P.O. Box 25336
  Alexandria, Virginia 22313

The text of this book is set in Century Old Style; display type is Helvetica and Gill Sans. The paper is 70 pound Warrenflo Gloss supplied by Stanford Paper Company. Typesetting by Intergraphics, Inc., Alexandria, Virginia. Color separation by Lanman Progressive, Washington, D.C. Printed and bound by Ringier America, New Berlin, Wisconsin.